Sampler Book 3, Ontario in Colour Photos, Saving Our History One Photo at a Time

Photography by Barbara Raué

Series Name: Cruising Ontario

Sampling from several towns

Each photo I take that precedes a demolition, or a natural disaster such as a tornado or a fire, is meeting this aim of mine of Saving Our History One Photo at a Time. There are more than 100 towns already photographed which you can visit without moving from your comfortable chair in your living room. Dream about what it was like in those by-gone days. Dream about what it was like to live in a mansion like one of these. Where would you like to travel to next?

Cover: 445 Talbot Street West, Aylmer, Page 44

Table of Contents

Elora, Ontario – My Top 5 Picks

Elmira, Ontario – My Top 7 Picks

St. Jacobs and area, Ontario – My Top 7 Picks

Linwood and Erbsville, Ontario – My Top 6 Picks

Wellesley, Ontario – My Top 6 Picks

Listowel, Ontario – My Top 6 Picks

Palmerston, Ontario – My Top 7 Picks

Dorchester to Aylmer, Ontario – My Top 6 Picks

Aylmer, Ontario – My Top 10 Picks

Drayton, Ontario and area – My Top 6 Picks

Tillsonburg, Ontario – My Top 5 Picks

Arthur, Ontario – My Top 9 Picks

Rockwood, Ontario – My Top 4 Picks

Acton, Ontario – My Top 8 Picks

Orillia, Ontario – My Top 5 Picks

Elora, Ontario – My Top 5 Picks

Elora is located in Wellington County on the Grand River and is about twenty kilometers north of Guelph, and twenty kilometers northeast of Kitchener-Waterloo.

Elora was founded in 1832 by Captain William Gilkison, a British officer recently returned from India. Gilkison named the community after his brother's ship, which was itself inspired by the Elora Caves near Aurangabad, Maharashtra, India.

The Elora Gorge, located at the western edge of the village, is one of the most scenic areas in Southern Ontario with its limestone cliffs descending 80 feet into the Grand and Irvine rivers where small caves, rapids, falls and quiet waters beckon visitors.

At the foot of Mill Street stands the Elora Mill, one of the few early Ontario five-storey grist mills still in existence.

David Boyle, born in Scotland in 1842, came to Canada in 1856 and settled in this area. As a local school teacher, he began an extensive collection of native artifacts and became an archaeological authority. In 1886, Boyle was appointed the first curator of the Provincial Archaeological Museum in Toronto. He was dedicated to the study and retention of artifacts and he initiated an active programme of excavation and acquisition. Through his work on Ontario prehistory, Boyle gained international recognition as a leading Canadian archaeologist and anthropologist.

When Elora first established itself as an agricultural supply center in the mid-nineteenth century, farmers coming from the north were greeted by a wagon and carriage factory, a lumber yard, blacksmith shops, and a farm implement enterprise.

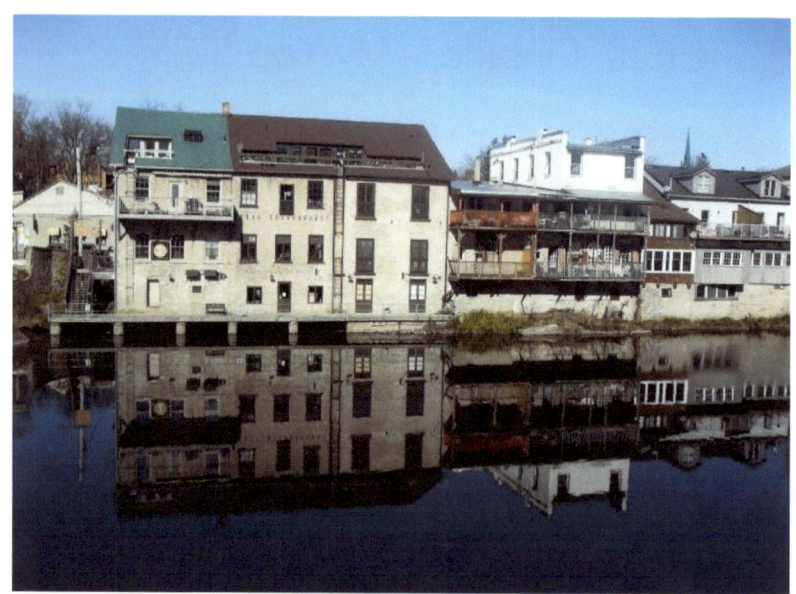

Reflections

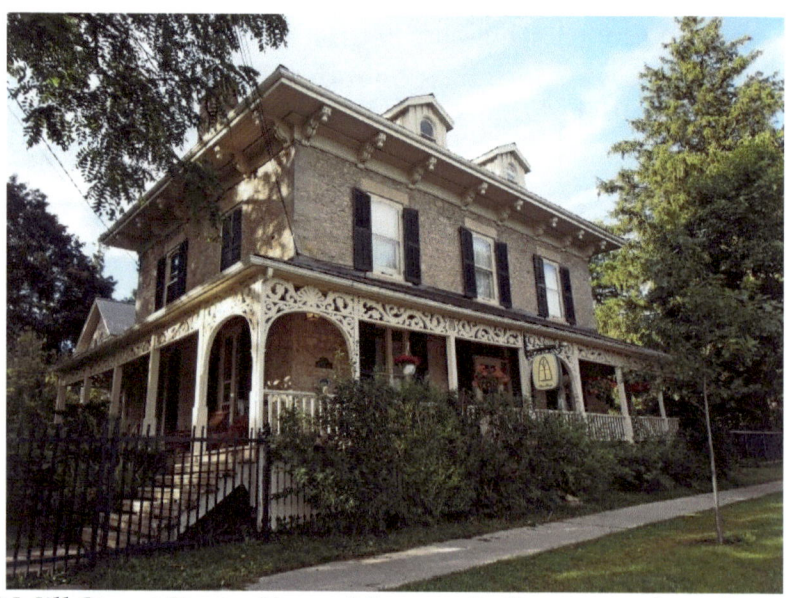

120 Mill Street East – Drew House - Italianate style – dormers in attic, single cornice brackets, wraparound verandah with bric-a-brac

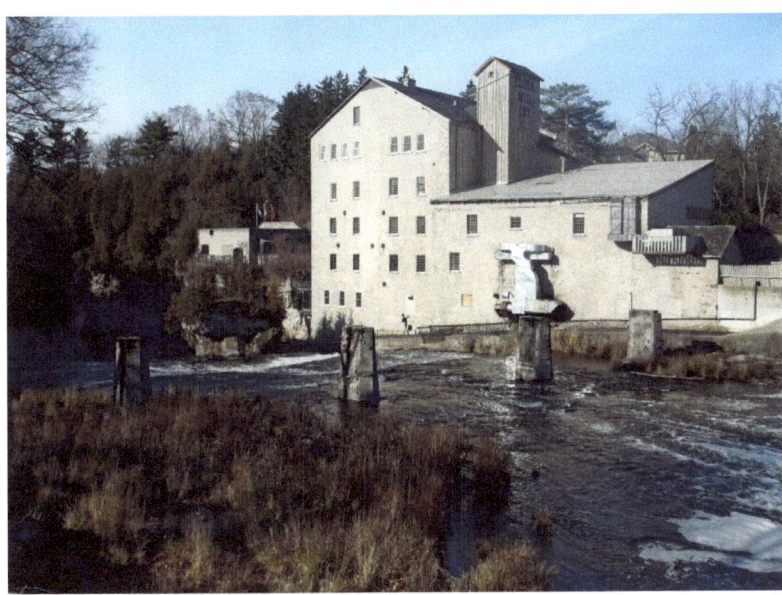

Elora Mill Inn - Towering 100 feet above the thundering falls of the Grand River, the Mill at Elora has stood for over 150 years as a symbol of what the combined energies of man and nature can achieve. The Mill was rebuilt mostly of stone after a fire in 1870.

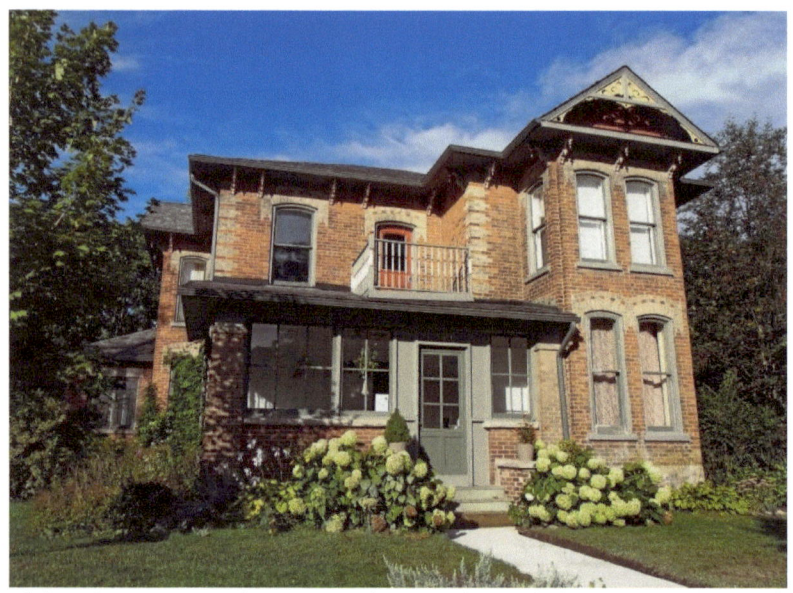

Geddes Street – Italianate – hipped roof, 2-storey tower-like bay topped with pediment with verge board trim, corner quoins, cornice brackets, voussoirs, dichromatic brickwork

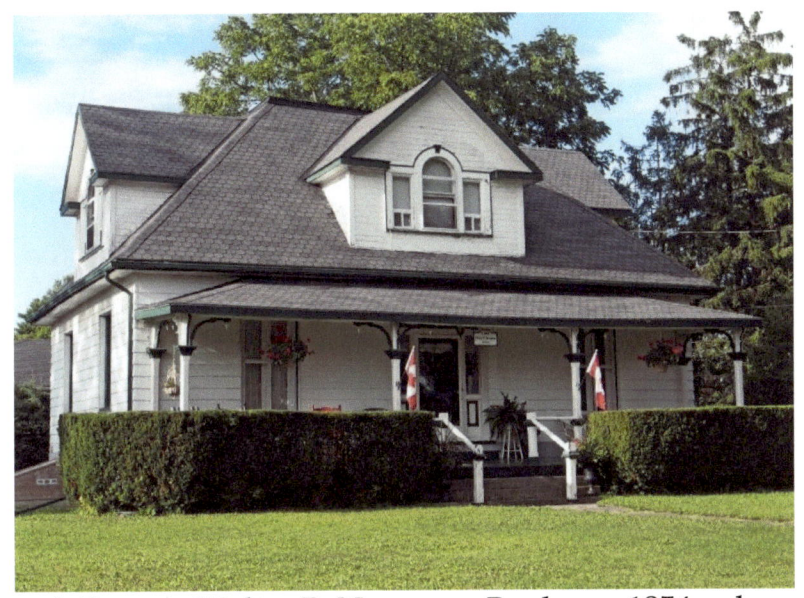

Church Street – Walter P. Newman, Banker c. 1854 – dormers in steeply pitched hip roof, Palladian window in dormer

Elmira, Ontario – My Top 7 Picks

Elmira is the largest community within the Township of Woolwich in the Regional Municipality of Waterloo and is located 15 kilometers (9 miles) to the north of the city of Waterloo.

The land comprising Woolwich Township originally belonged to the Huron and then the Mohawk Indians. The first settlers arrived in Woolwich Township in the late eighteenth century. In 1798, William Wallace, one of the first settlers in the area, was deeded 86,078 acres of land on the Grand River for a cost of $16,364.

In 1806, Wallace sold the major portion of his tract to Mennonites. Benjamin Eby, the secretary of the Germany Company came to the area with his friend Henry Brubacher. The young men liked Wallace's Woolwich. Eby returned to Pennsylvania where he formed a land company. The following year, he returned with a barrel of silver dollars, and the Musselmans, Martins, Hoffmans, and Gingerichs to settle in the area. Wallace sold the Germany Company 45,185 acres of land at $1.00 an acre.

In 1834, Edward Bristow became one of Elmira's first settlers when he purchased 53 acres of land here for 50 cents per acre. A community by the name of Bristow's Corners was in existence in 1839 when a post office was assigned there. In 1853 the community was renamed Elmira. In the 1850s, German settlers moved into the community, including Oswald, Esche, Steffen and Tresinger. Like most of the township, the primary settlers in the Elmira area were Mennonites who still form a significant proportion of the population today. The town still retains much of its traditional Pennsylvania Dutch character.

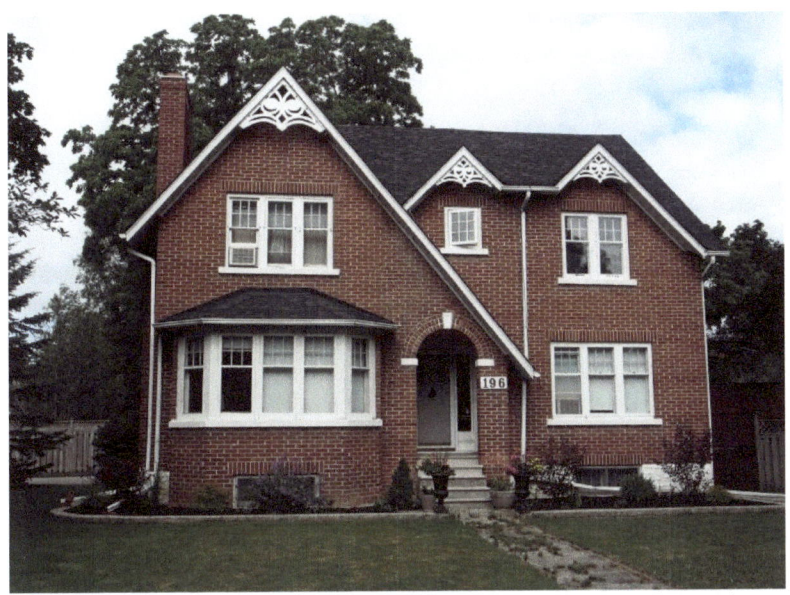

196 Arthur Street South – Gothic Revival, verge board trim – Elmira Book 1

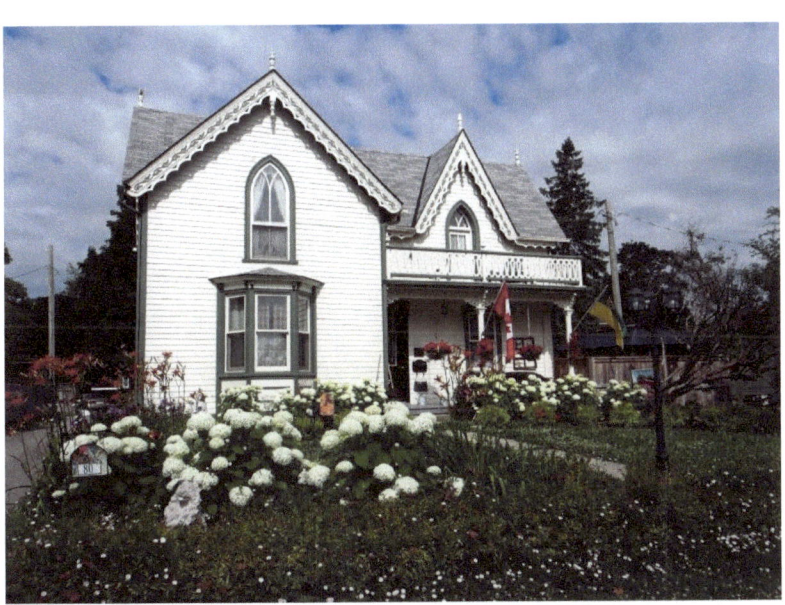

80 Arthur Street South – Gothic Revival, verge board trim – Elmira Book 1

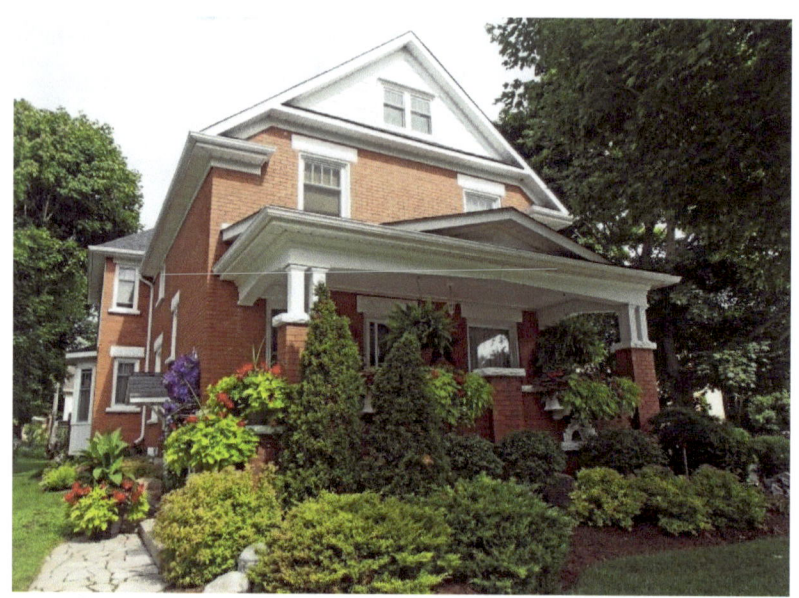

24 Queen Street – Edwardian – Elmira Book 1

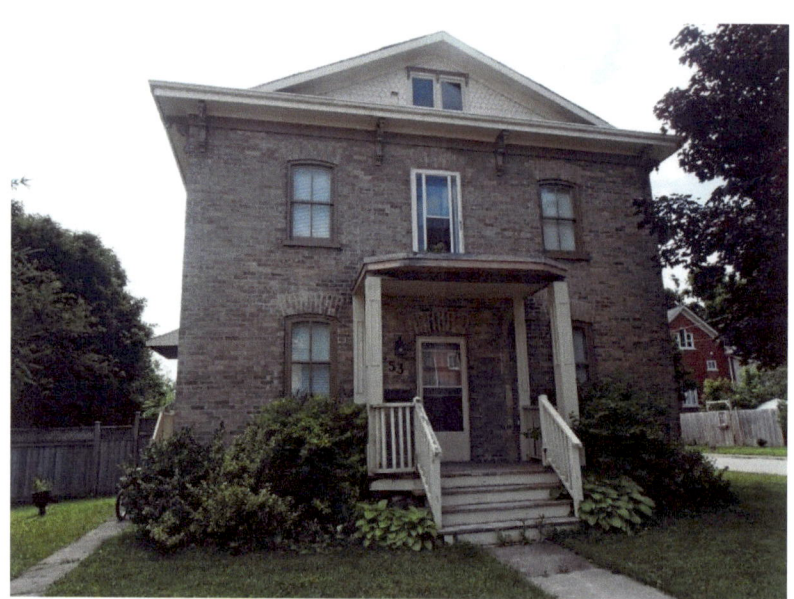

53 Memorial Avenue – Italianate – dormer – Elmira Book 1

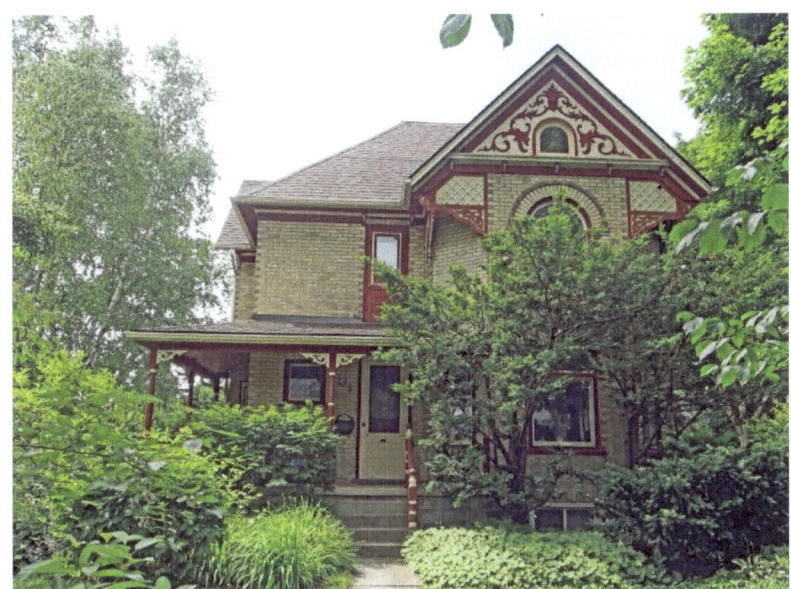

5 Park Avenue – decorative gable, Romanesque style arch on second floor window – Elmira Book 2

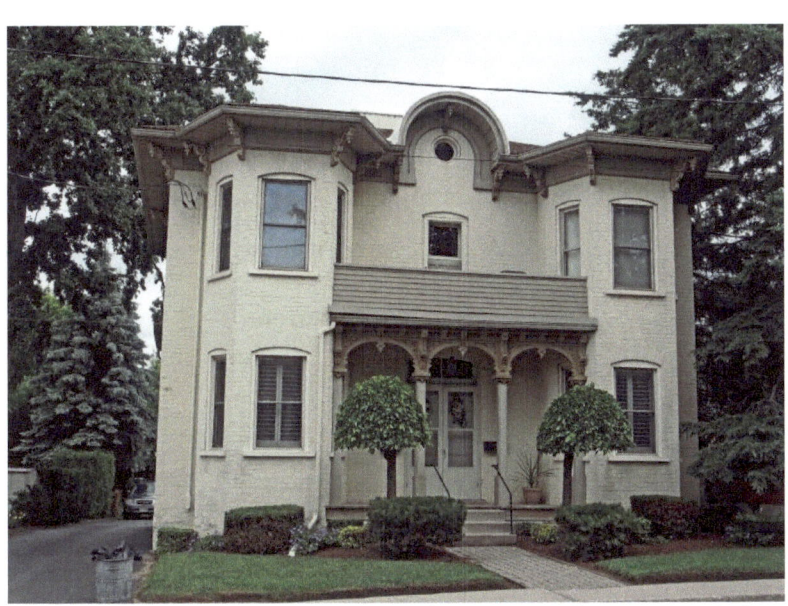

42 Church Street West – Italianate – Elmira Book 2

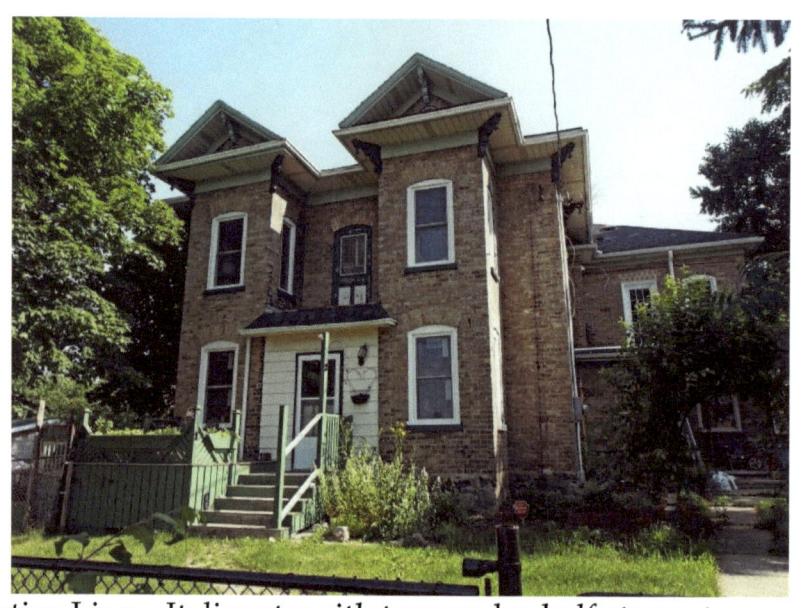

Martins Line – Italianate with two-and-a-half storey tower-like bays, cornice brackets
– Elmira Book 2

St. Jacobs and area, Ontario – My Top 7 Picks

St. Jacobs is located in southwest Ontario just north of Waterloo. It is a popular location for tourism due to its Mennonite heritage and retail focus. The Conestogo River, which powered the village's original gristmill, runs through the village.

St. Jacobs was settled in 1819 and was first known as "Jakobstettel" which means "Jacob's Village" or "James's Village". The *St.* was added to the name simply to make it sound more pleasing and the pluralization was in honor of the combined efforts of Jacob C. Snider and his son, Jacob C. Snider, Jr., founders of the village.

St. Jacobs' developed as a thriving business community throughout the 1800s with such businesses as a felt factory, tannery, glue factory, flour mill, saw mill, and furniture factory. The village served the needs of surrounding pioneer farm settlements. Situated on Arthur Road, St. Jacobs boasted four hotels by 1852. One of these - Benjamin's Restaurant and Inn - is still operating today.

St. Jacobs features dozens of artisans in historic buildings, such as the Country Mill, Village Silos, Mill Shed, and the Old Factory. Visitors may watch artisans make pottery, quilts, designer clothes, jewelry, glass vases, woven wall hangings, tiffany lamps, stained glass doors, miniature doll houses, and more. There are also two blacksmith shops to visit. The Visitor Centre is a Mennonite interpretation center providing information and education on the Mennonite people in the community.

St. Clements, Heidelberg, Crosshill and Bamberg are communities in the Township of Wellesley.

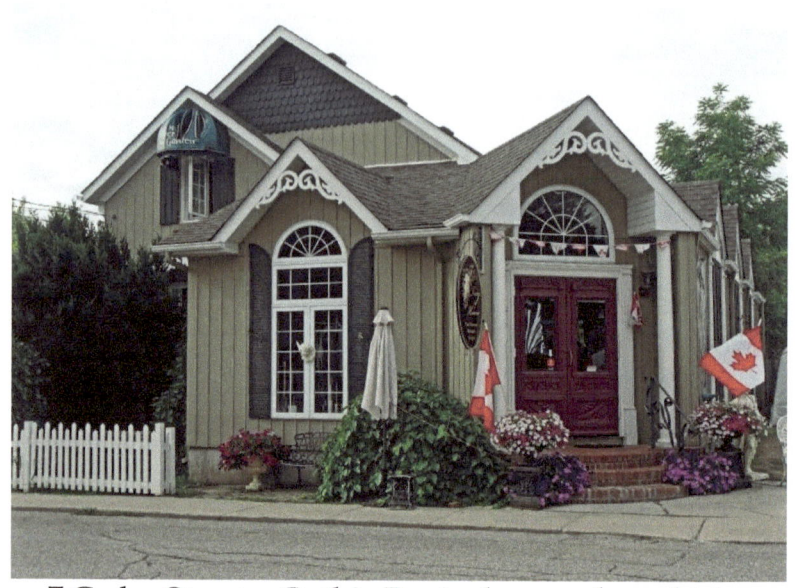

7 Cedar Street – Gothic Revival, verge board trim

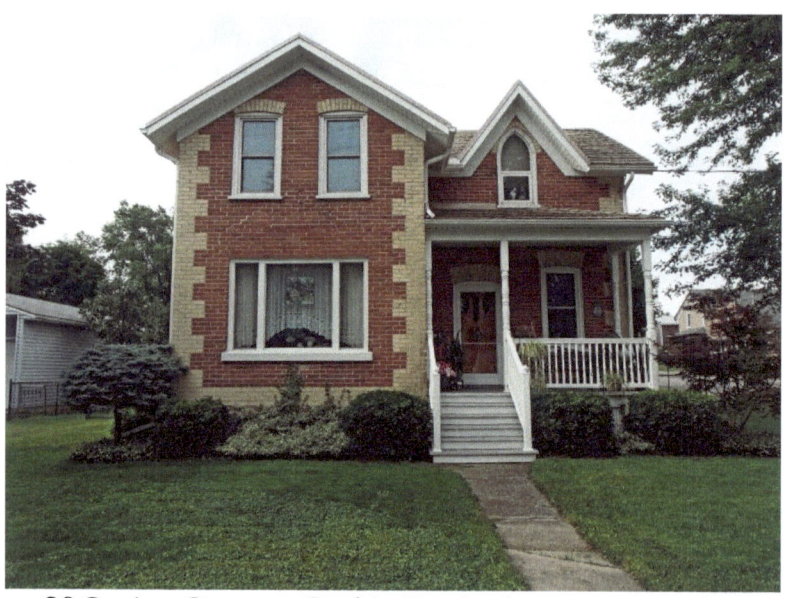

29 Spring Street – Gothic Revival – corner quoins

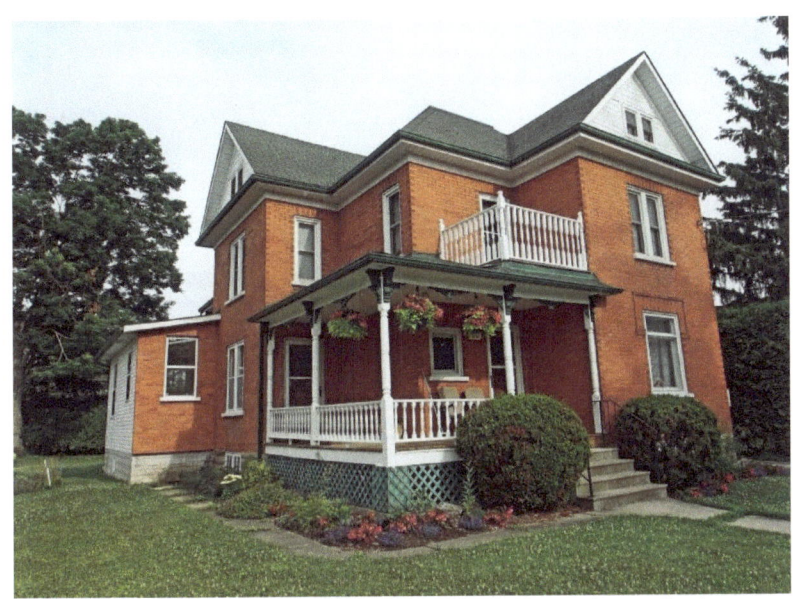

20 Isabella Street – Edwardian, second floor balcony

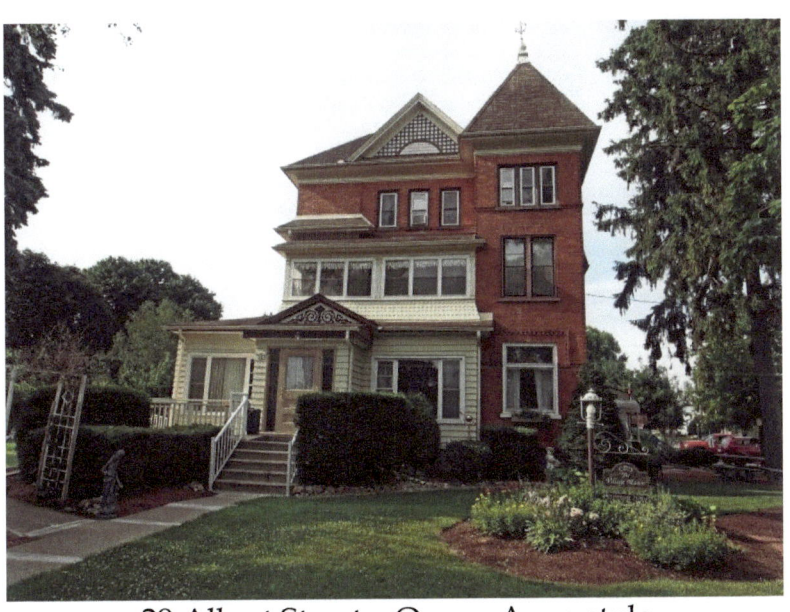

29 Albert Street – Queen Anne style

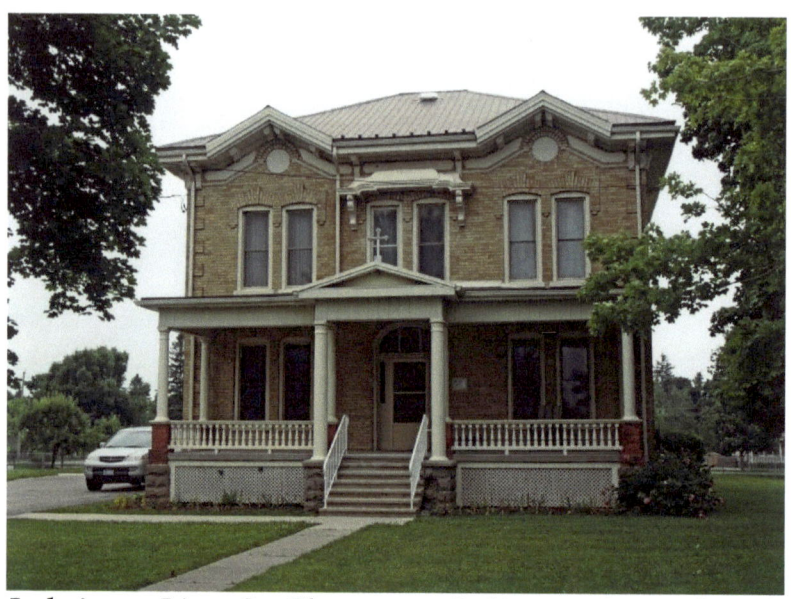

Lobsinger Line, St. Clements – Italianate, hipped roof, pediment

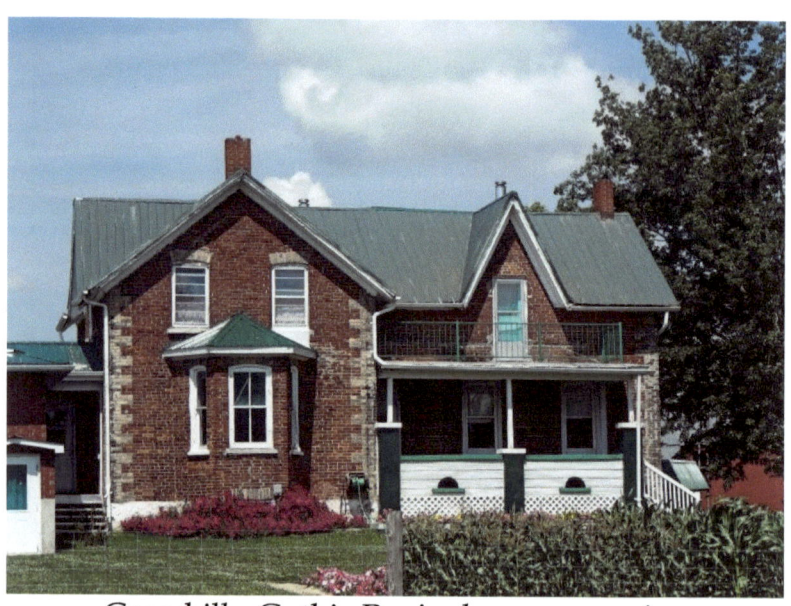

Crosshill - Gothic Revival, corner quoins

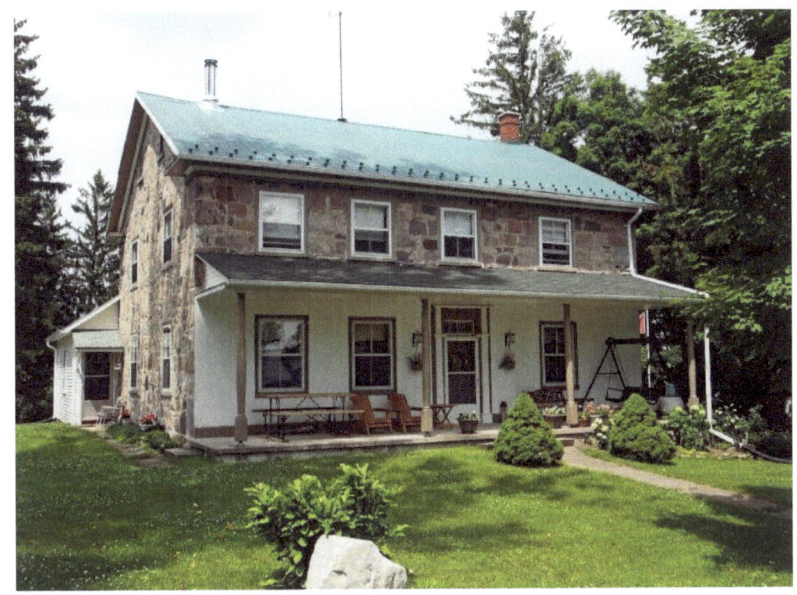

Bamberg - Stone house

Linwood and Erbsville, Ontario – My Top 6 Picks

The Township of Wellesley is the rural, north-western township of the Regional Municipality of Waterloo. The township comprises the communities of Bamberg, Crosshill, Hawkesville, Heidelberg, Kingwood, Knight's Corners, Linwood, Macton, St. Clements, Wallenstein and Wellesley.

The country scenery and rolling hills, along with its small town feel, have transformed the township into a commuter town with the population travelling into the nearby cities of Kitchener and Waterloo for work.

Wellesley Township was surveyed in 1842, but settlers were in this area long before. The town of Wellesley's original name was *Schmidtsville*, derived from its founding settler, John Schmidt. In 1851, the town was renamed *Wellesley* after Richard Wellesley, 1st Marquess Wellesley, the eldest brother of Arthur Wellesley, 1st Duke of Wellington. The community quickly grew to be the largest economic center in rural Waterloo Region with a wood mill, feed mill, grain mill (which still stands after being constructed in 1856), leather tanner, cheese factory, restaurants and housing, and many other businesses that also brought much trade to the town from the nearby farms and farming villages.

When the Waterloo County boundaries were established in 1852 they included the townships of Waterloo, Wellesley, Wilmot, Woolwich, and North Dumfries.

The first library in Wellesley Village was incorporated in 1900. The current branch is located in the former S.S. No. 16 Wellesley Township public school building. The school closed its doors in 1967.

Macton is on the northern boundary line of Wellesley Township, three miles northeast of Linwood, twenty miles northwest of Berlin, three miles east of Wallenstein. Macton was settled later than St. Clements, mostly by Irish people.

Erbsville is located about five miles west of Kitchener.

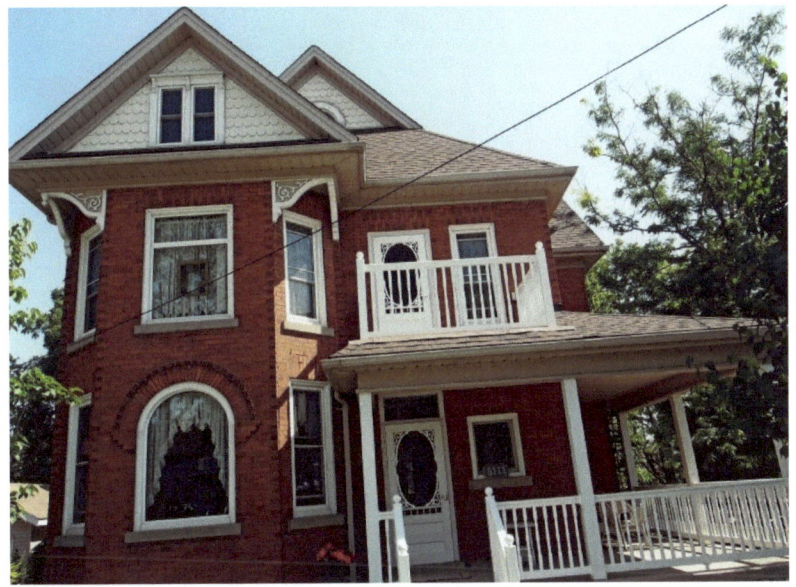

Ament Line, Linwood – Edwardian, fretwork

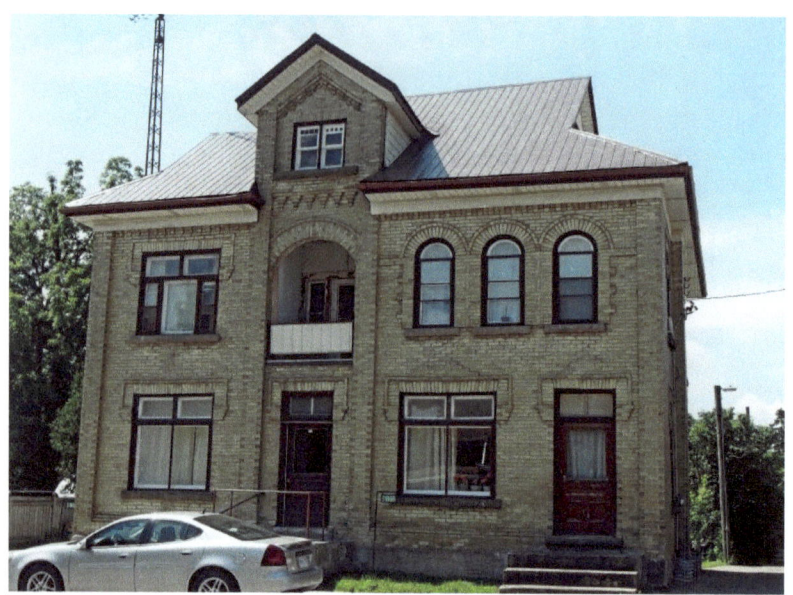

5186 Ament Line, Linwood – Italianate, with two-and-a-half storey tower-like structure, arched window voussoirs, dentil molding

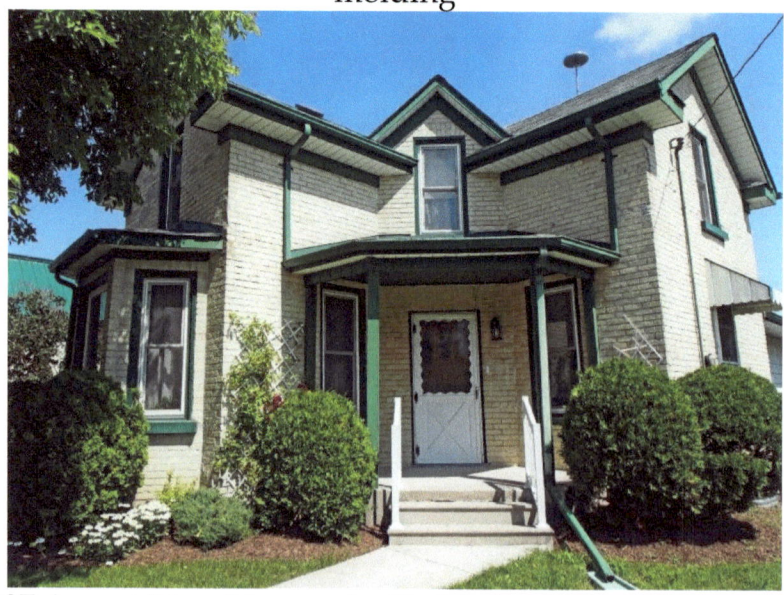

5297 Ament Line, Linwood – Gothic Revival, unique shape, cornice return on end gable

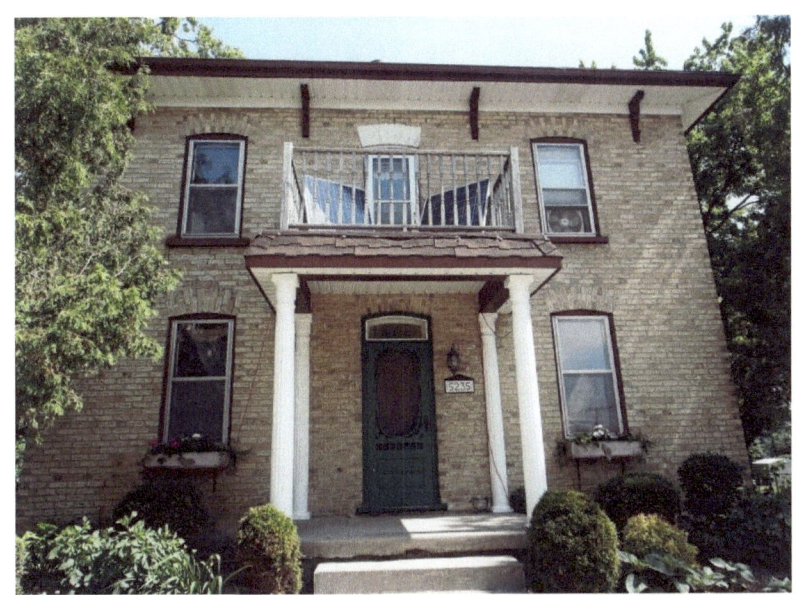

5235 Ament Line, Linwood – Italianate – cornice brackets, balcony on second floor

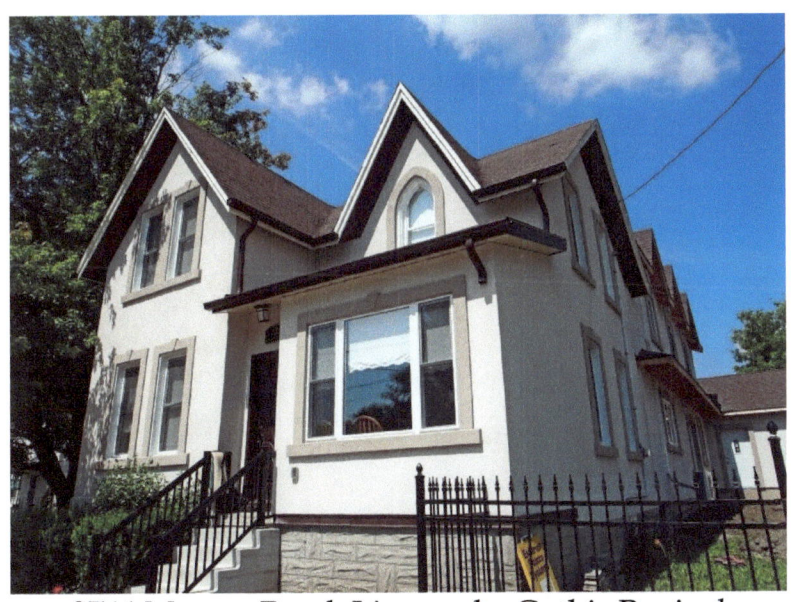

3744 Manser Road, Linwood – Gothic Revival

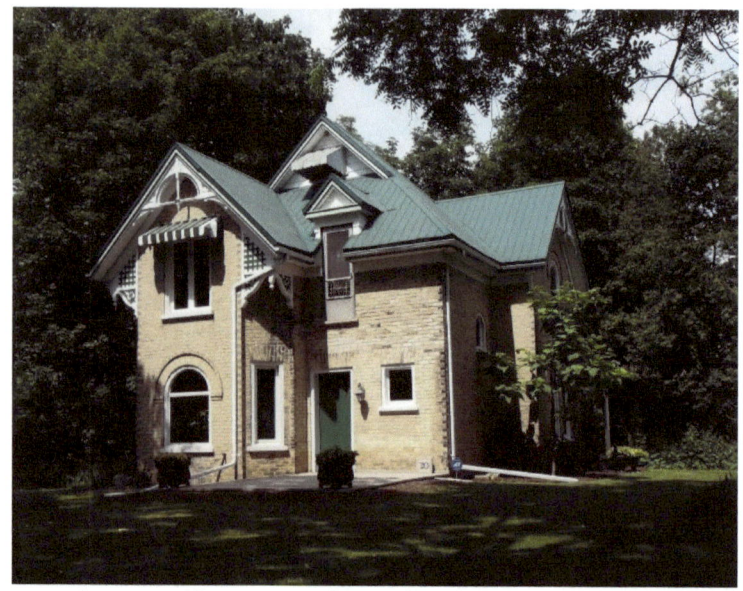

Queen Anne style, verge board trim on gables - Erbsville

Wellesley, Ontario – My Top 6 Picks

The Township of Wellesley is the rural, north-western township of the Regional Municipality of Waterloo. The township comprises the communities of Bamberg, Crosshill, Hawkesville, Heidelberg, Kingwood, Knight's Corners, Linwood, Macton, St. Clements, Wallenstein and Wellesley.

The country scenery and rolling hills, along with its small town feel, have transformed the township into a commuter town with the population travelling into the nearby cities of Kitchener and Waterloo for work.

Wellesley Township was surveyed in 1842, but settlers were in this area long before. The town of Wellesley's original name was *Schmidtsville*, derived from its founding settler, John Schmidt. In 1851, the town was renamed *Wellesley* after Richard Wellesley, 1st Marquess Wellesley, the eldest brother of Arthur Wellesley, 1st Duke of Wellington. The community quickly grew to be the largest economic center in rural Waterloo Region with a wood mill, feed mill, grain mill (which still stands after being constructed in 1856), leather tanner, cheese factory, restaurants and housing, and many other businesses that also brought much trade to the town from the nearby farms and farming villages.

When the Waterloo County boundaries were established in 1852 they included the townships of Waterloo, Wellesley, Wilmot, Woolwich, and North Dumfries.

The first library in Wellesley Village was incorporated in 1900. The current branch is located in the former S.S. No. 16 Wellesley Township public school building. The school closed its doors in 1967.

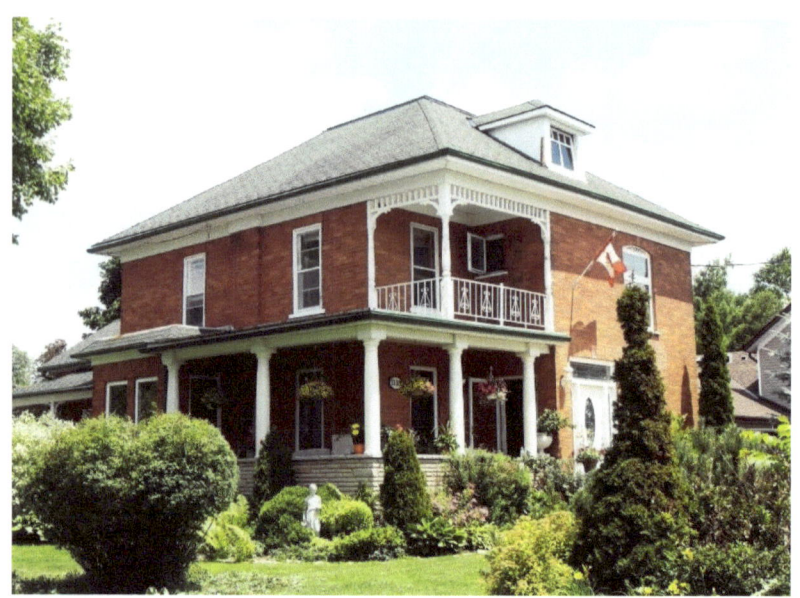

1115 Queen's Bush Road – Italianate style, hipped roof, dormer

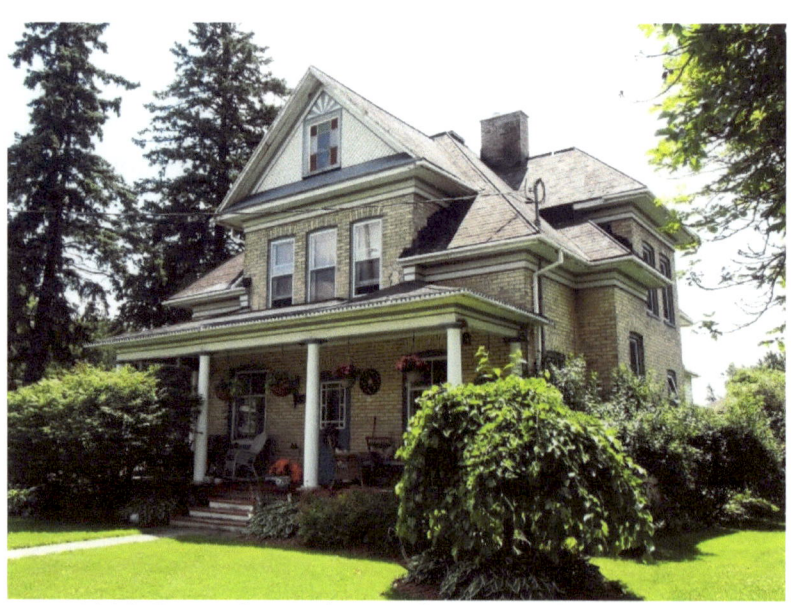

1110 Queen's Bush Road – Queen Anne style

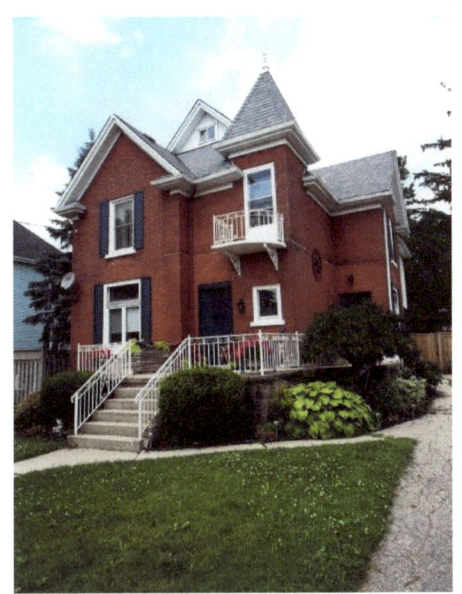

1155 Queen's Bush Road - Queen Anne style

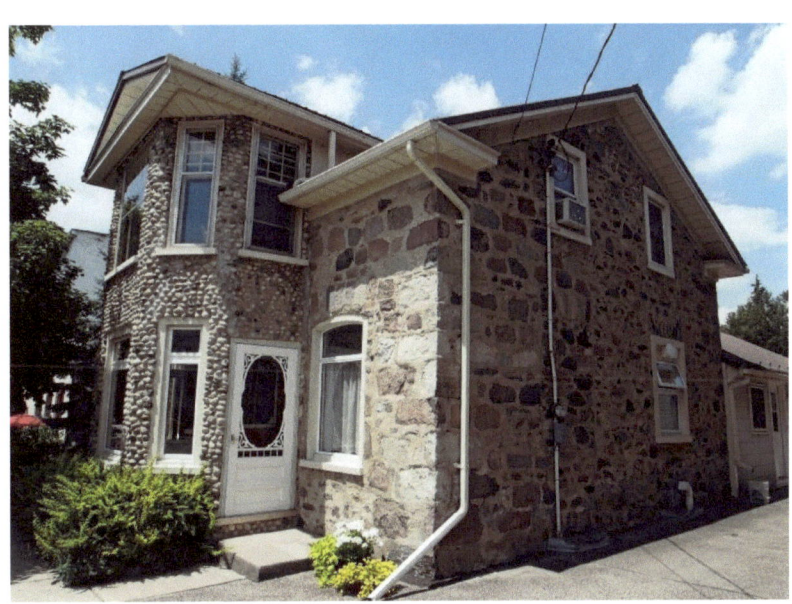

1189 Queen's Bush Road – stone architecture, cornice return on end gable

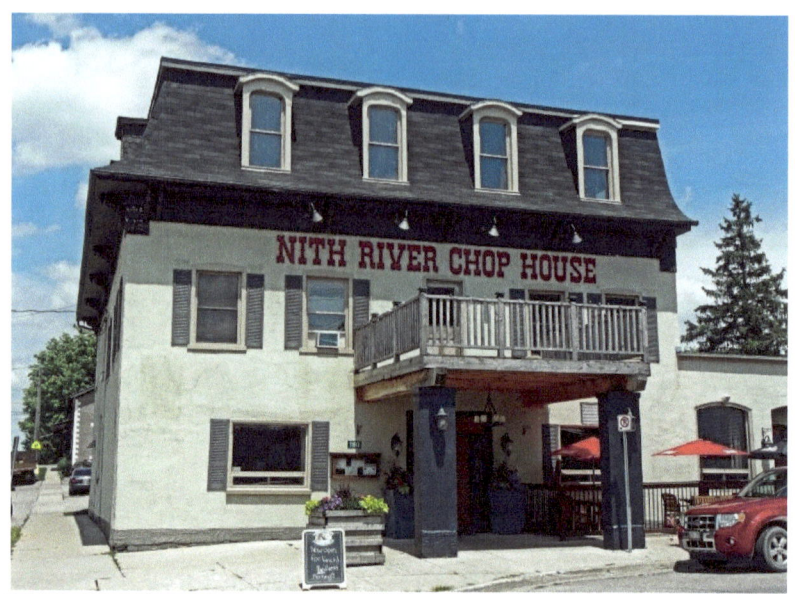

1193 Queen's Bush Road – Nith River Chop House - Second Empire style – mansard roof with dormers

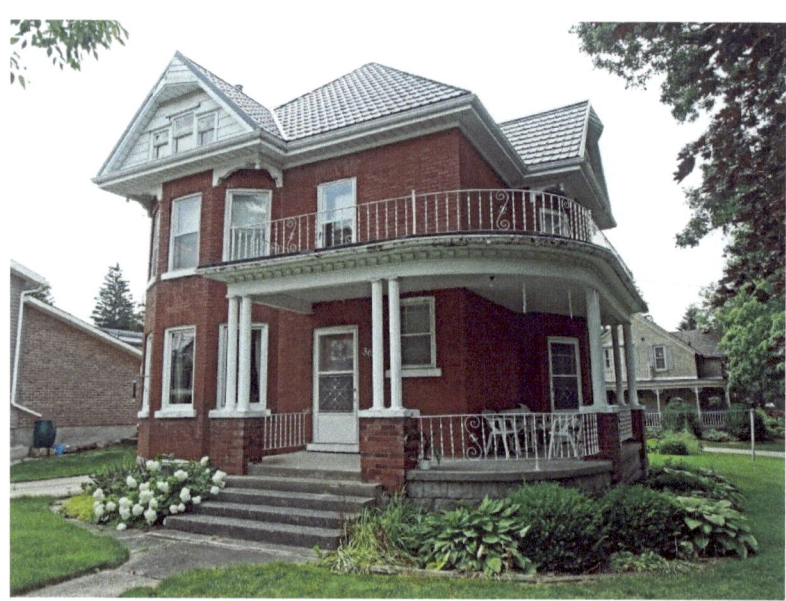

Nafziger Road – Edwardian – wraparound verandahs on both storeys, Palladian window, fretwork

Listowel, Ontario – My Top 6 Picks

Listowel is located in the municipality of North Perth, northwest of Kitchener/Waterloo, and west of Elmira on Highway 86.

Settler John Binning arrived in 1857 and was the first to create a permanent residence in the area. The community was originally named Mapleton, but the name was changed when a post office was established. The new name was chosen by a government official and refers to Listowel, Ireland (a market town in County Kerry situated on the River Feale, twenty-eight kilometers, or seventeen miles, from the county town, Tralee.) The majority of early settlers were of Protestant Irish origin.

In 1871 the Wellington, Grey and Bruce Railway extended its line to Listowel. It was joined in 1873 by a second railway, the Stratford and Huron Railway, and Listowel became an important shipping point. The population doubled when industries, including a woolen mill, a sawmill, a planing mill and a tannery, were established. In 1891 the Morris, Field, Rogers Company Ltd began to manufacture Morris pianos in Listowel.

In 1907, hydroelectric and telephone services came to the town with the Princess cinema. During World War II the theatre was renamed the Capitol and remains Canada's oldest operating cinema.

The Campbell Soup Company was a major local employer for 48 years, operating a frozen, foodservice and specialty food plant in Listowel. The factory closed in April 2008. The surrounding area is mostly agricultural land located on the Perth Plain, dominated by the beef and pork industries.

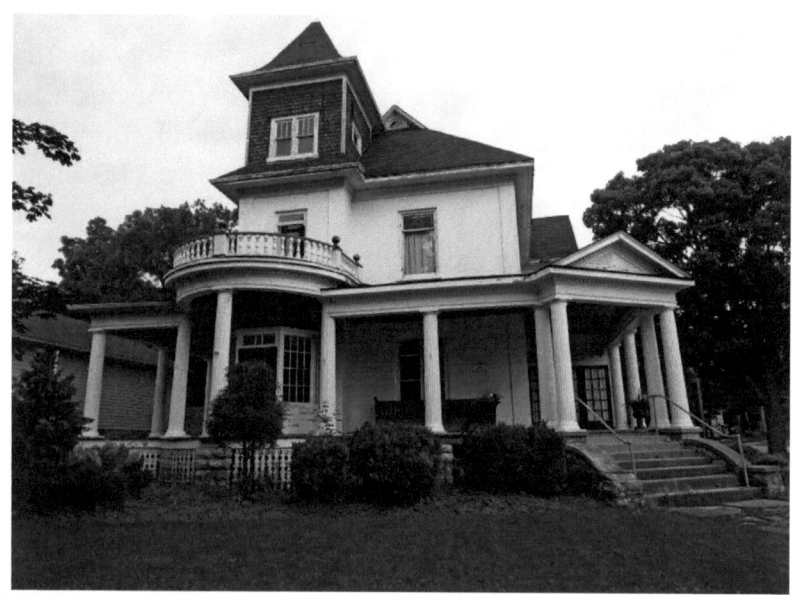

215 Binning Street West – two-storey, white brick, tower, dormer – originally this was a full three storeys high with a Mansard roof; a fire in 1922 damaged the upper level and a new roof was added in the Queen Anne style; spindle railing around circular balcony, Doric pillars, pediment

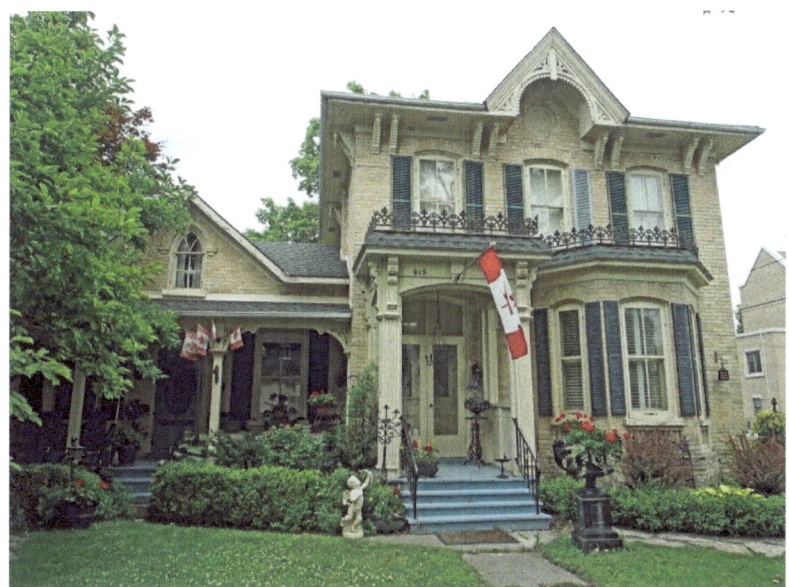

415 Inkerman Street West – built in two distinct styles – the larger east half is Italianate with paired cornice brackets, iron cresting above porch and above bay window, decorative gable; the smaller west half is rural Ontario design with a verandah

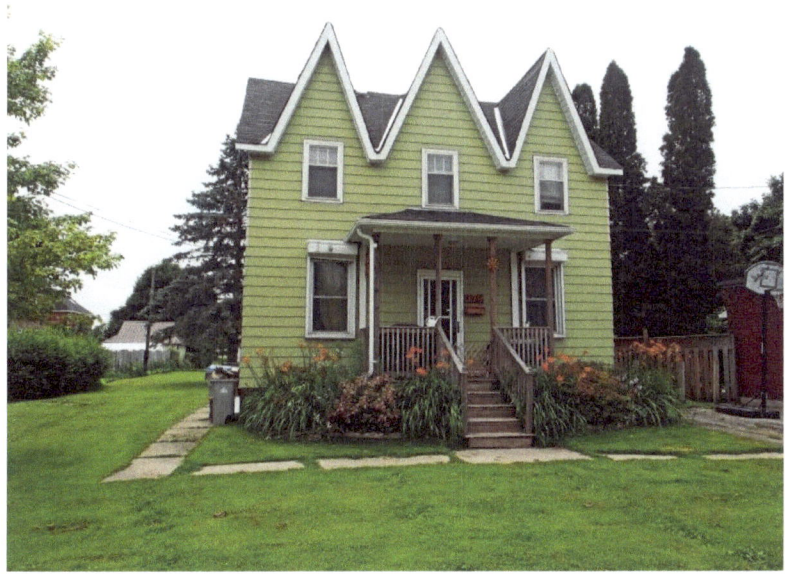

370 Inkerman Street West – triple gable Gothic Revival

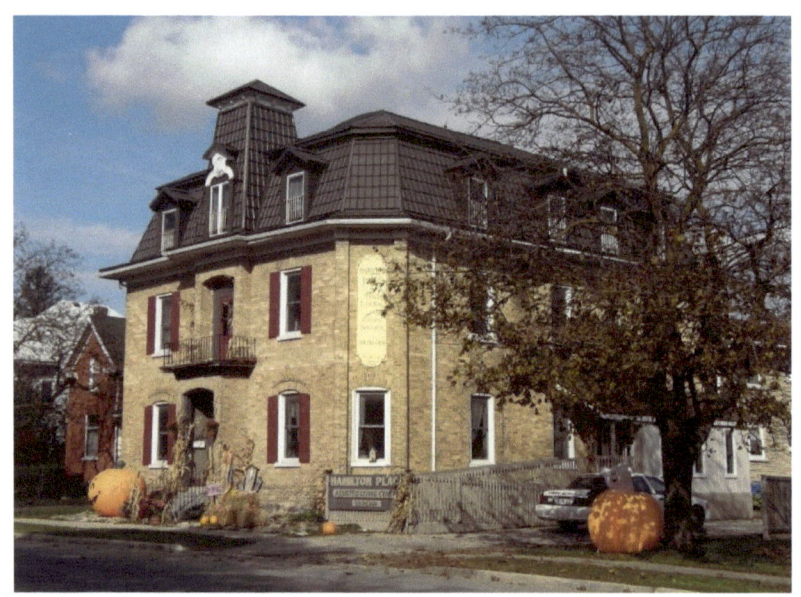

469 Main Street West – Second Empire style, Mansard roof, dormers with window hoods, built of Wallace brick – was once on edge of town and operated as the Last Chance Hotel – last chance for a drink before leaving town

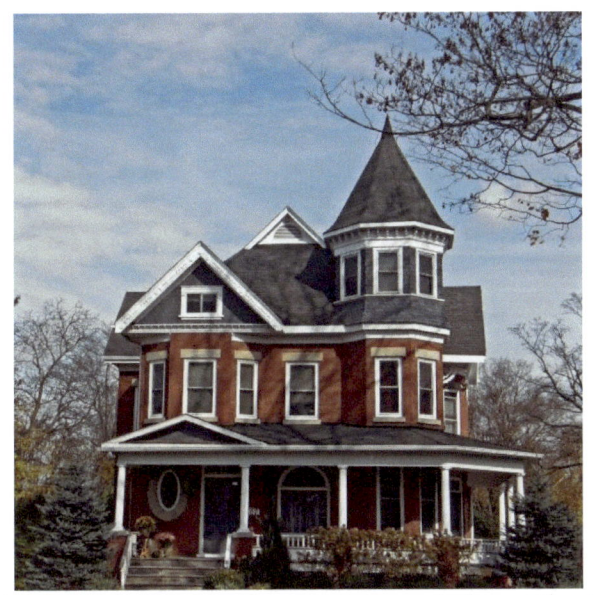

507 Main Street West – Queen Anne style with plenty of windows, chimneys and gables

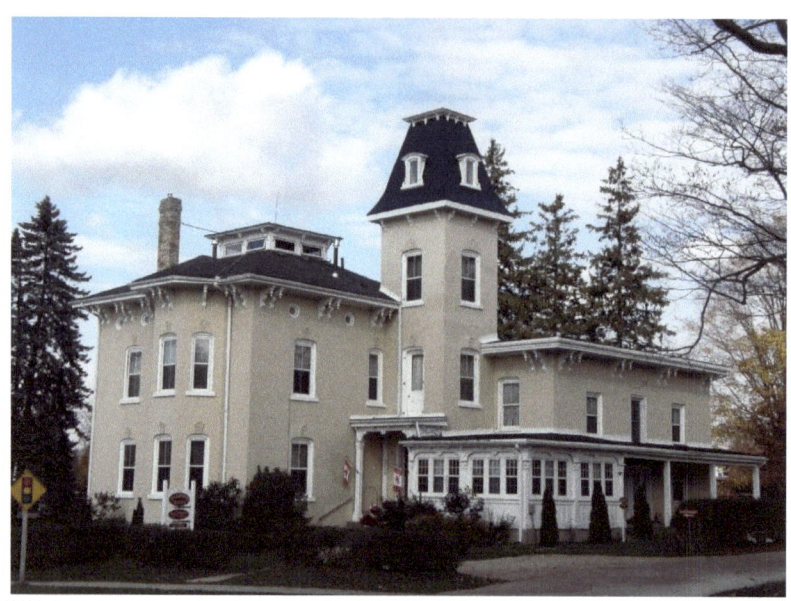

555 Main Street West – Italianate with four-storey tower, belvedere on roof – site of Listowel's first settler John Binning's log cabin; the present house is one of the oldest in town, built in 1860, tower and front half added in 1870

Palmerston, Ontario – My Top 7 Picks

Palmerston is located in Wellington County, west of Arthur, northeast of Listowel, and northwest of Kitchener and Waterloo.

The opening in 1871 of a station on the main line of the Wellington, Grey and Bruce Railway soon to be completed from Guelph to Southampton, provided the nucleus around which a community developed. In its original concept the railroad was to run from Guelph to Harriston and would not have gone through Palmerston. Listowel needed to be linked to the railroad and it was decided to bend the route toward Listowel. It was also decided that a yard with maintenance shops would be needed. As soon as the railroad decided where it would build, people started buying property around the area for businesses and homes.

Thomas McDowell was the first settler in 1854 on the site. In 1872 McDowell and William Thompson who owned adjoining land, began selling town lots and by 1873 the community had 150 inhabitants.

In 1873 a branch line to Listowel was completed and a post office called Palmerston, named after Lord Palmerston, a celebrated English statesman, was opened.

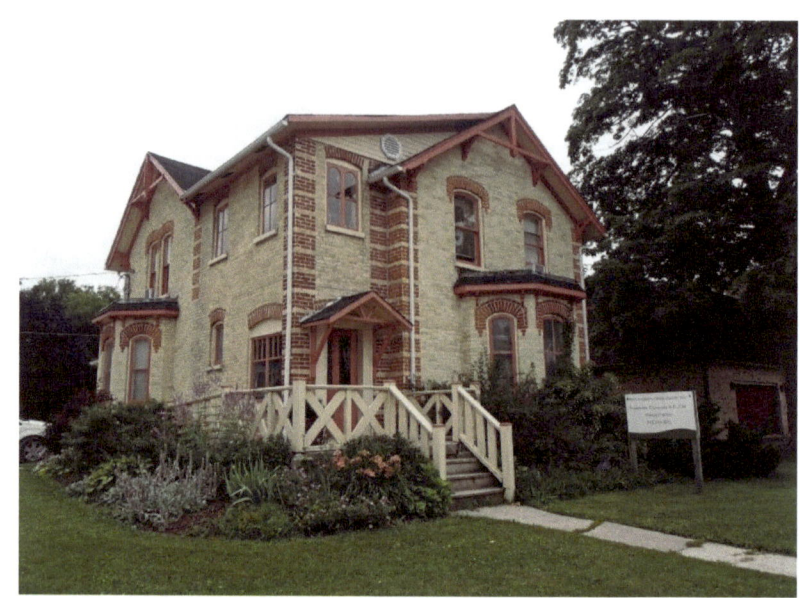

Main Street – Gothic Revival, dichromatic brickwork, bay windows, corner quoins

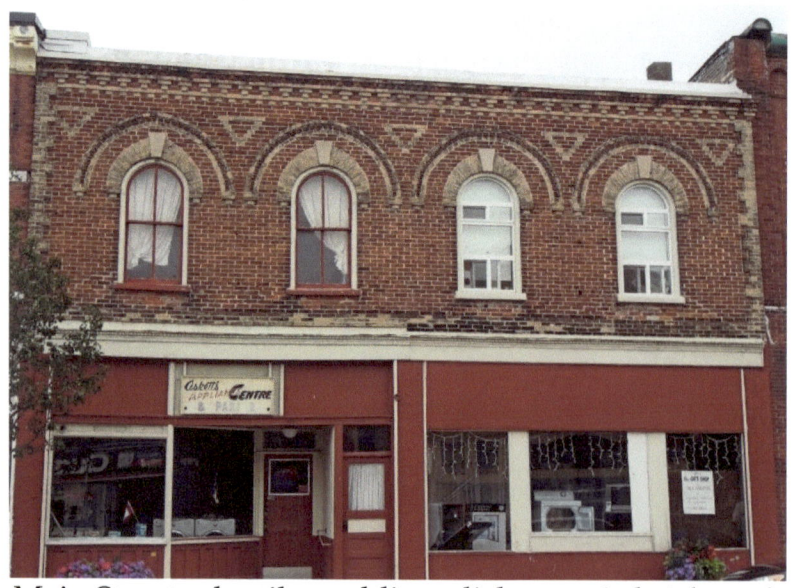

Main Street - dentil moulding, dichromatic brickwork

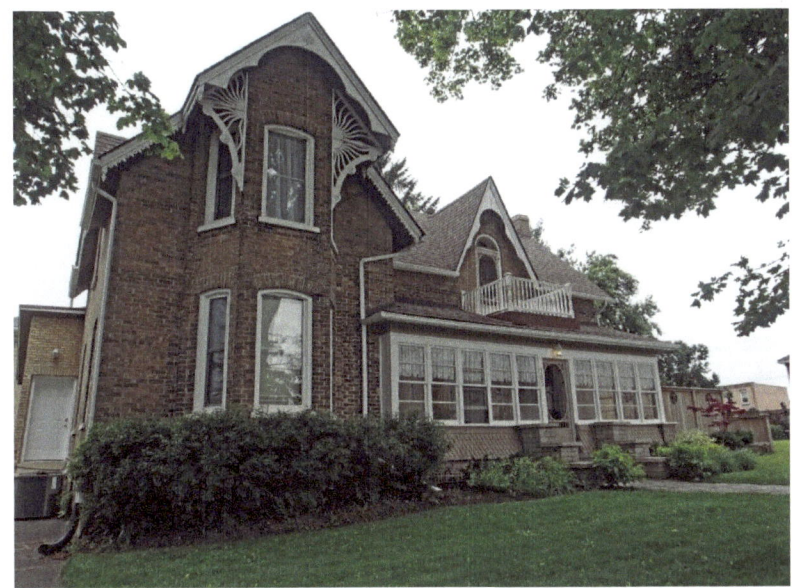

Bell Street – Gothic Revival, verge board trim, fretwork

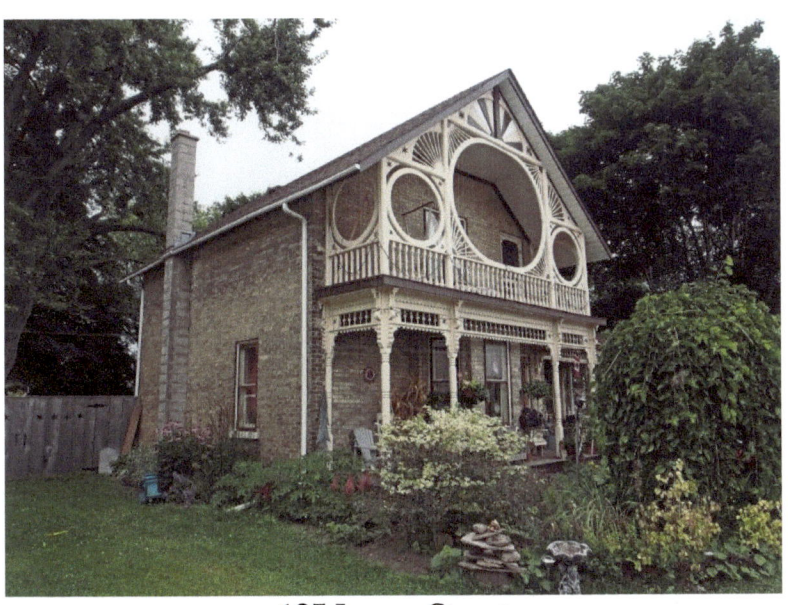

125 James Street

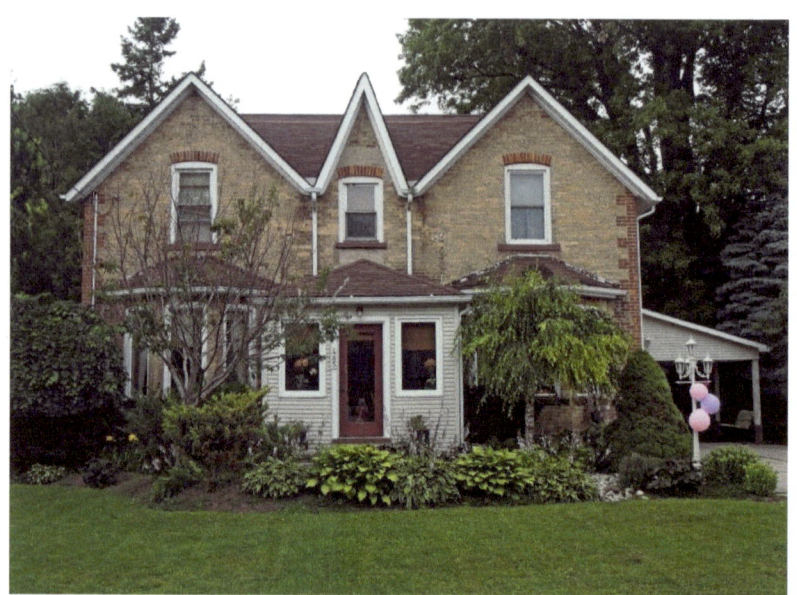

485 King Street – triple gable Gothic Revival, dichromatic brickwork, corner quoins, bay windows

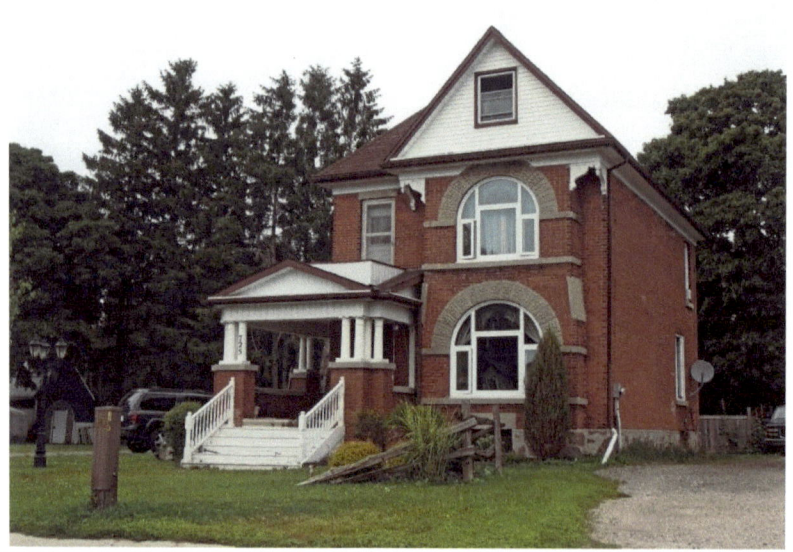

725 King Street – Edwardian – Romanesque style window voussoirs, fretwork, pediment above verandah

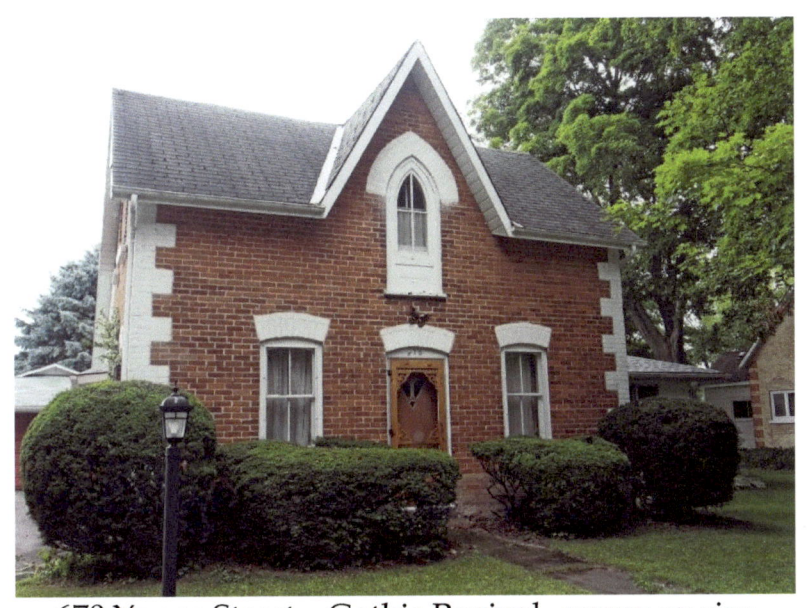

670 Yonge Street – Gothic Revival, corner quoins

Dorchester to Aylmer, Ontario – My Top 6 Picks

Thames Centre is a municipality in Middlesex County located in southwestern Ontario a few kilometers east of London. Communities in the township include: Avon, Belton, Cherry Grove, Crampton, Cobble Hill, Derwent, Devizes, **Dorchester**, Evelyn, Fanshawe Lake, Friendly Corners, Gladstone, **Harrietsville**, Kelly Station, **Mossley**, Nilestown, Oliver, Putnam, Salmonville, Silvermoon, Thorndale, Three Bridges, and Wellburn. **Dorchester** is the residential and commercial core of the township.

Mossley

Until 1840 the Mossley area was an untouched wilderness of pines, maples, and beeches. The first settlers from England, Scotland, Ireland and Wales worked hard to clear the land for farming. They came with few tools but great hope for a better way of life, and they prospered. In the 1800s this area was known simply as "The Corners". In 1865 John Henry Amos opened a general store and was the first postmaster. The name Mossley was chosen from two family names, the Mossips and the Lees. Mossley had a hotel, a cheese factory, a harness repair shop, and there were dressmakers and music teachers.

Malahide Township was named for Malahide Castle in Malahide, Ireland, birthplace of land grant administrator Colonel Thomas Talbot in 1810. The township comprises the communities of Candyville, Crossley-Hunter, Copenhagen, Dunboyne, Fairview, Glencolin, Grovesend, Jaffa, Kingsmill, Lakeview, Little Aylmer, Luton, **Lyons**, Mile Corner, Mount Salem, Mount Vernon, Ormond Beach, Orwell, **Port Bruce**, Seville, Springfield, Summers Corners and Waneeta Beach.

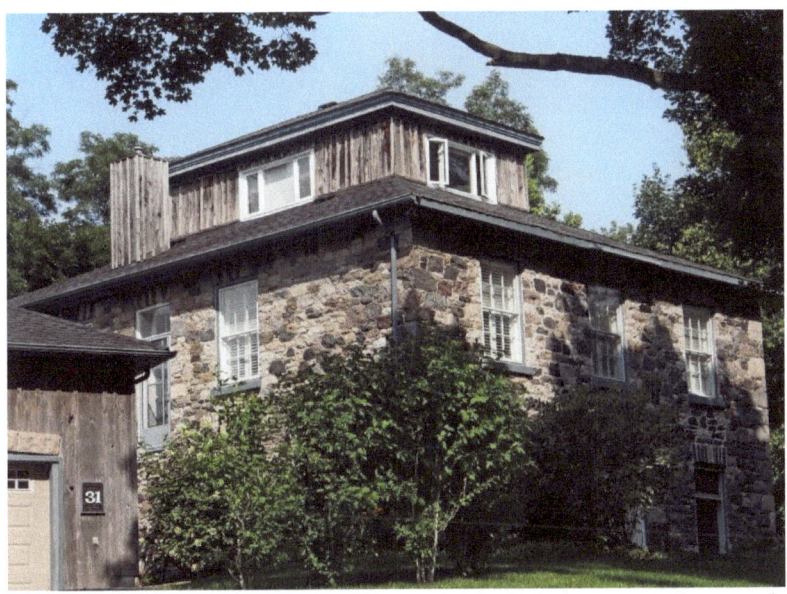

31 Mill Road, Dorchester - Mr. Cartwright's stone house built in 1866 with river and field stones with eighteen inch thick walls – Georgian style. There are ten main rooms. There is a "widow's walk" or belvedere on the roof with a view of the river from windows on all four sides.

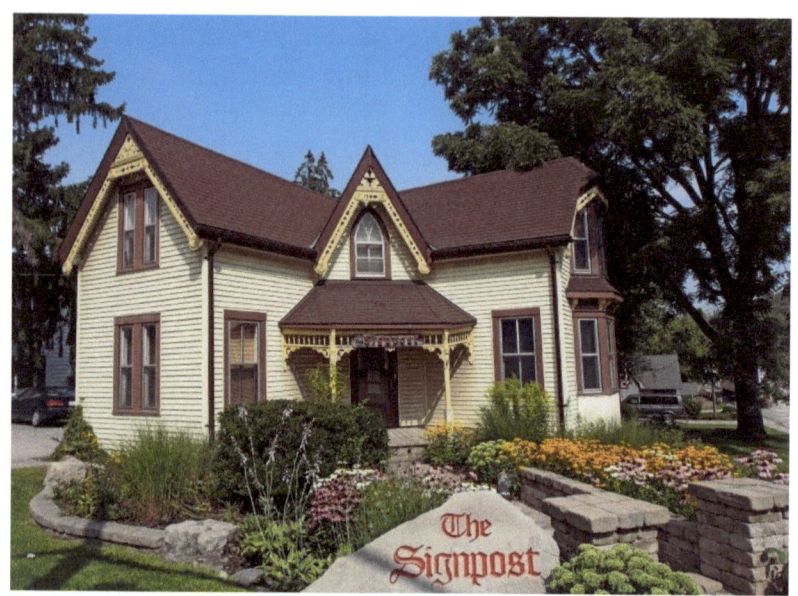

15 Bridge Street, Dorchester – The Signpost – Gothic Revival, verge board trim on gables

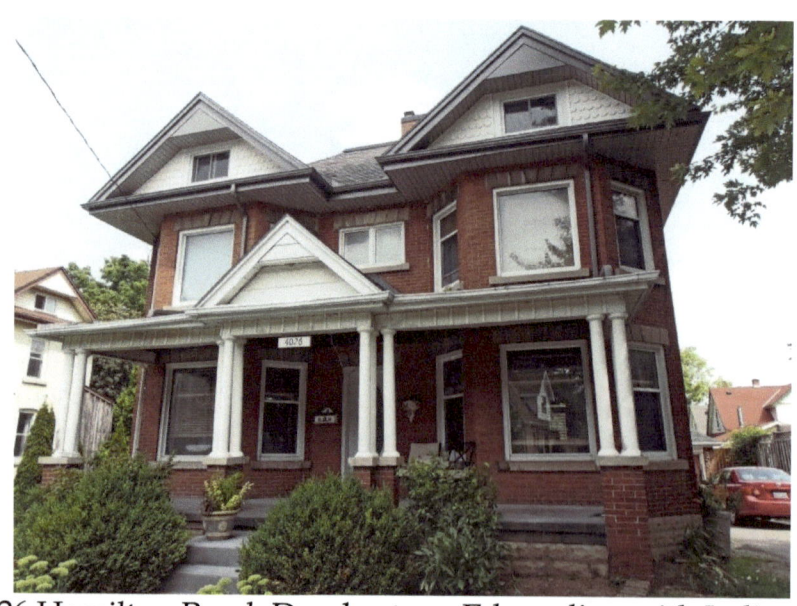

4026 Hamilton Road, Dorchester – Edwardian with Italianate features, two-storey bay window, pediment

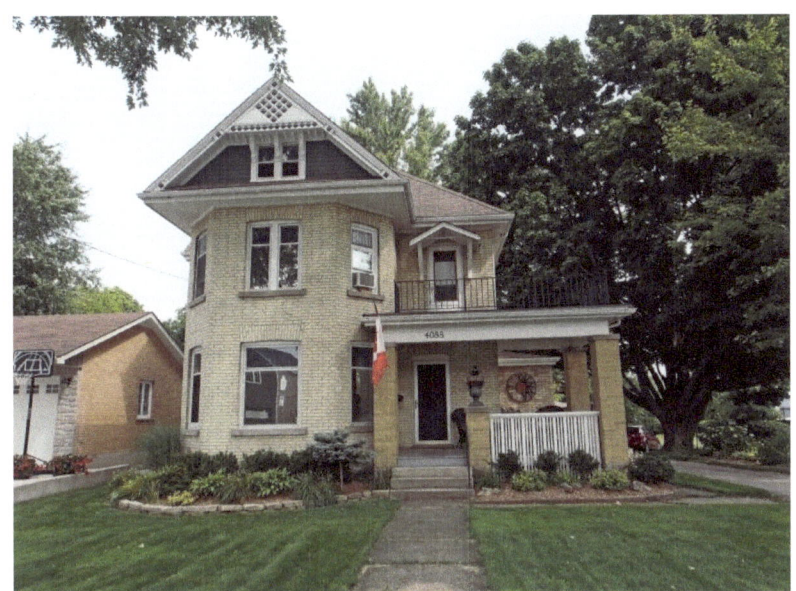

4088 Hamilton Road, Dorchester – Edwardian with two-and-a-half storey tower-like bay

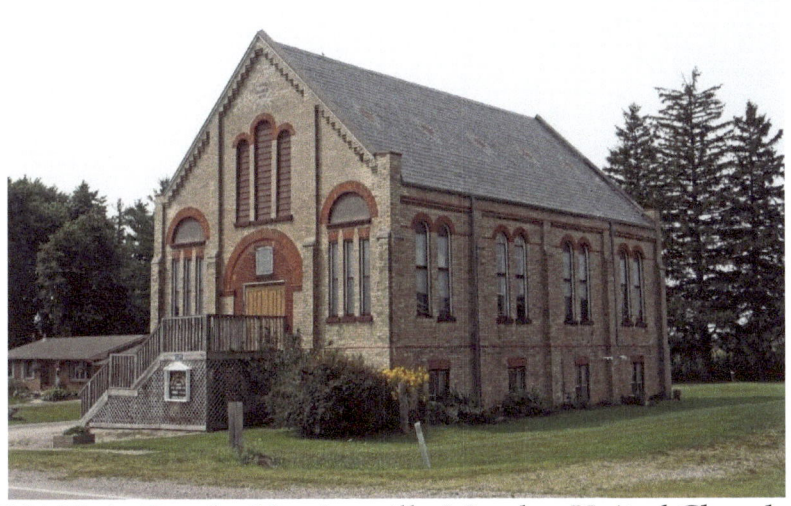

5391 Elgin Road – Harrietsville-Mossley United Church – former Methodist Church – 1896 – Gothic Revival, dichromatic brickwork, buttresses, dentil molding

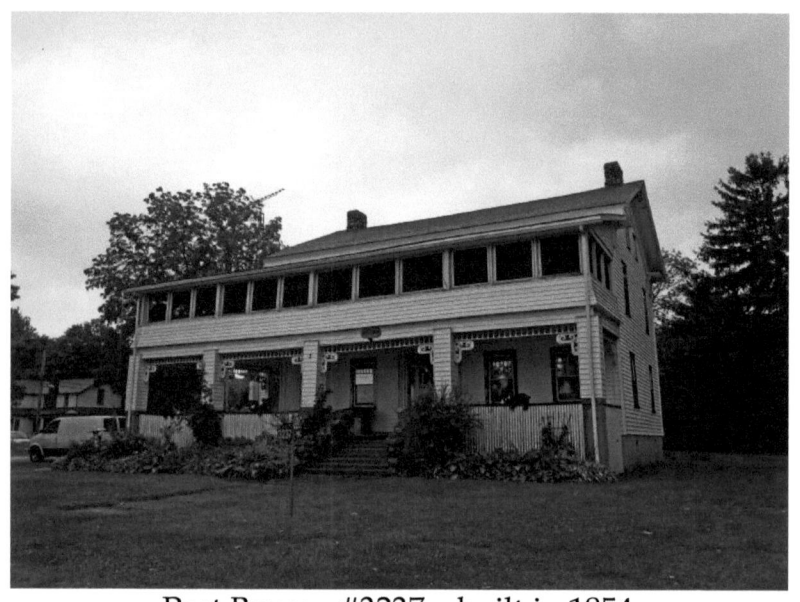

Port Bruce - #3237 – built in 1854

Aylmer, Ontario – My Top 10 Picks

Aylmer is located in southern Ontario just north of Lake Erie on Catfish Creek. It is 20 kilometers south of Highway 401. It is located on Highway 3 between St. Thomas to the west, and Tillsonburg to the east.

In October 1817, John Van Patter, an emigrant from New York State, obtained 200 acres of land and was the first settler on the site of Aylmer. During the 1830s a general store was opened and village lots sold.

Originally called Troy, in 1835 it was renamed Aylmer after Lord Aylmer, then Governor-in-Chief of British North America. By 1851 local enterprises included sawmills and flour-mills powered by water from Catfish Creek.

By the mid-1860s Aylmer, with easy access to Lake Erie, became the marketing center for a rich agricultural and timber producing area. Aylmer benefited greatly from the construction of the 145-mile Canada Air Line Railway from Glencoe to Fort Erie.

The coming of the Great Western Air Line railway in 1873 encouraged manufacturing and mills, a foundry, a pork-packing house, a milk-evaporating plant, and shoe factory were among the main establishments. An Airfield for training was established nearby in World War 2 which became the nucleus of the Ontario Police College.

The Aylmer Canning Factory was established in 1879; it packed peas, beans, cider, pickles, vinegar, sauces, meats and fruits.

Imperial Tobacco Canada built a plant in 1945. At its peak, it employed more than 600 full-time and seasonal workers. In its prime, the plant could store 110 million tons of tobacco and had an October to April production capacity of 100 million tons. Of this, 20 to 25 million tons were for export to other countries, making it one of Canada's leading exporters. The rest of the processed tobacco was shipped to Imperial's cigarette production plant in Guelph. After declining tobacco sales in Canada, Imperial began downsizing in the 1990s and closed in 2007.

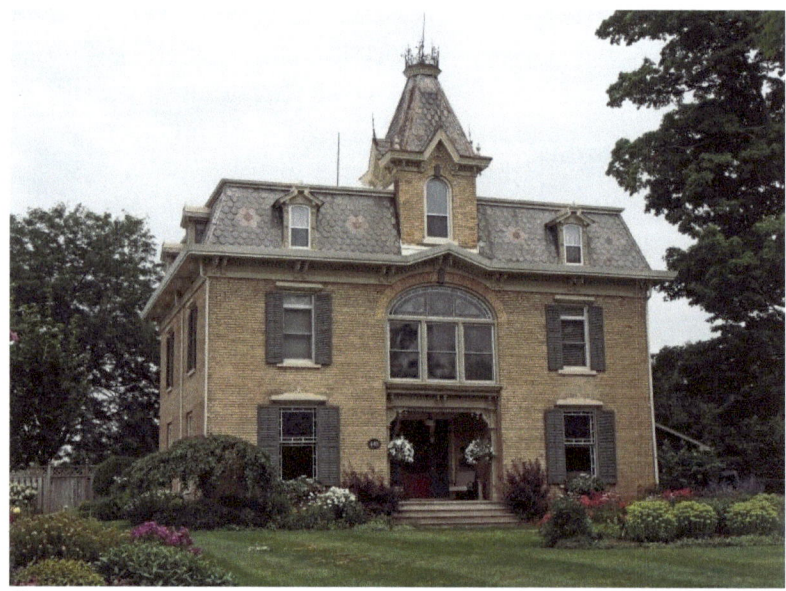

445 Talbot Street West – Second Empire style, mansard roof, iron cresting, window hoods on dormers – Aylmer Book 1

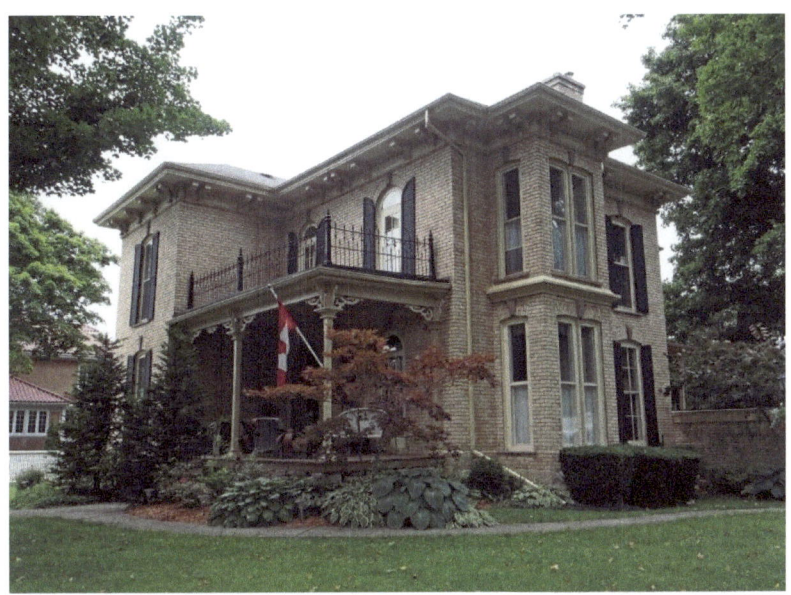

375 Talbot Street West – Italianate, cornice brackets, two-storey tower-like bays, balcony on second floor – Aylmer Book 1

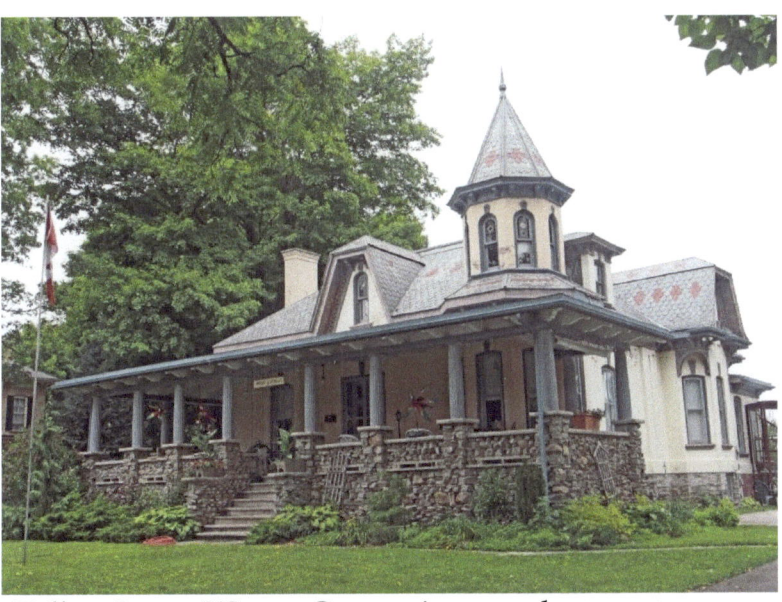

Talbot Street West – Queen Anne style, turret, trichromatic tile work – Aylmer Book 1

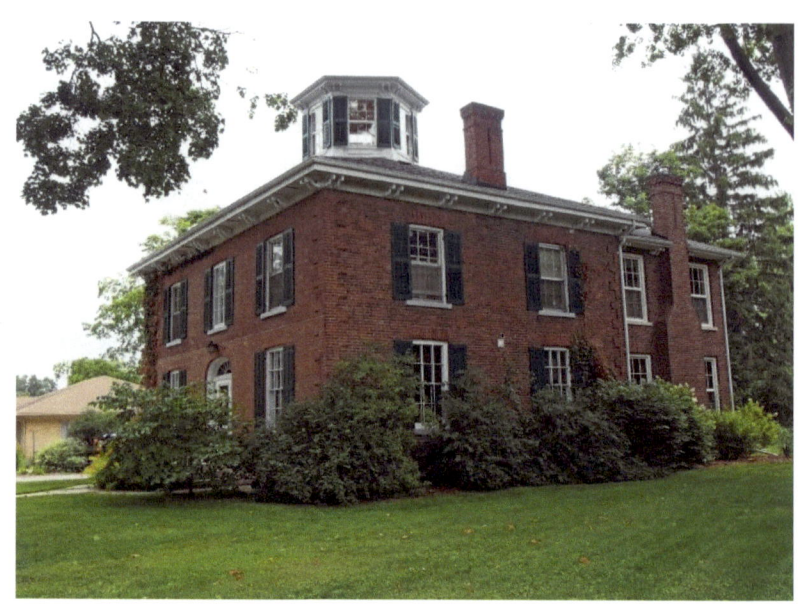

30 South Street – Georgian, belvedere on rooftop – Aylmer
Book 1

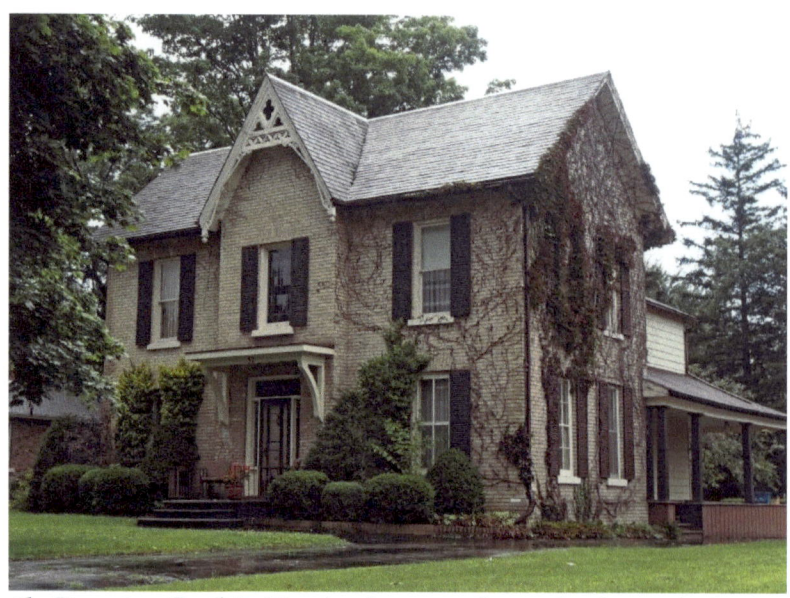

52 South Street – Gothic Revival, verge board trim – Aylmer
Book 1

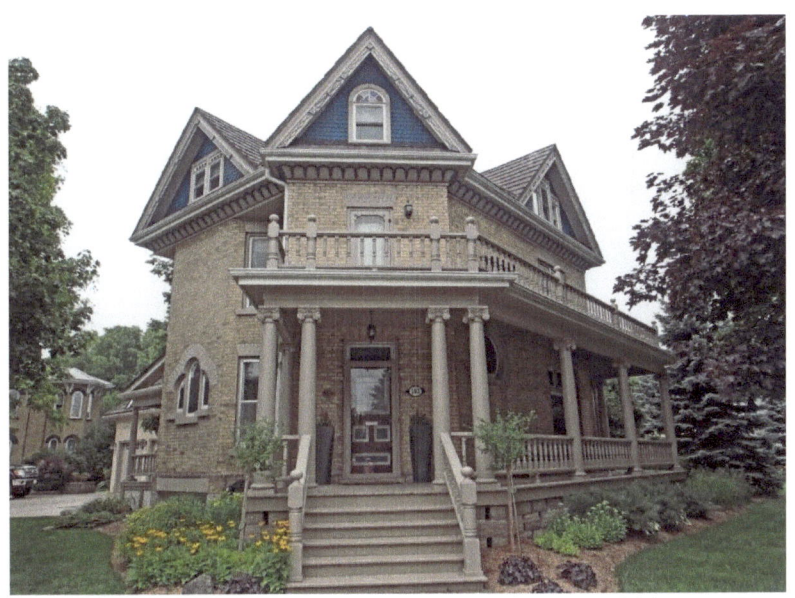

193 John Street South – Queen Anne style – c. 1899 - Ionic columns with scroll-like capitals – Aylmer Book 1

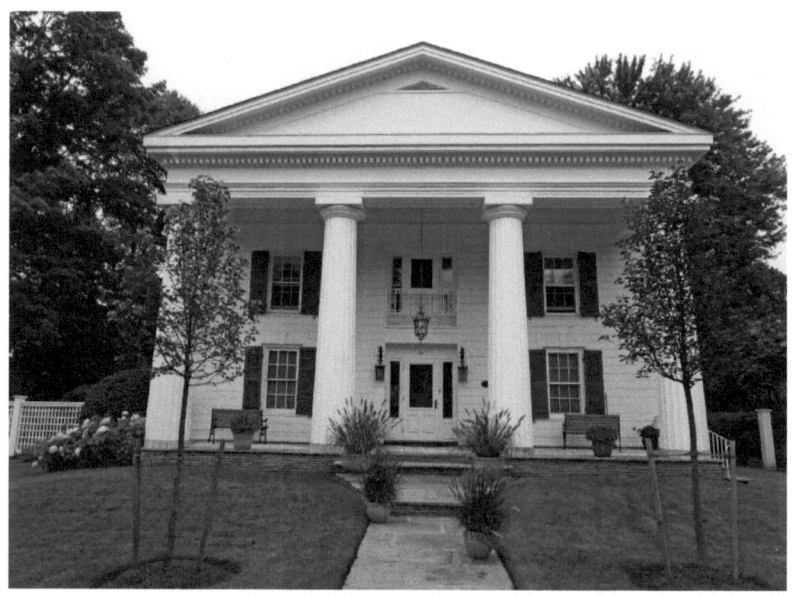

24 Pine Street – McLay-Minielly house built in 1853 in Classical Neo-Grecian (see Renaissance Revival style in appendix) architecture in frame construction of tongue and groove siding; entablature consisting of dentils, bands of moulding, frieze, and architrave; two-storey-high Doric pillars, pediment – Aylmer Book 2

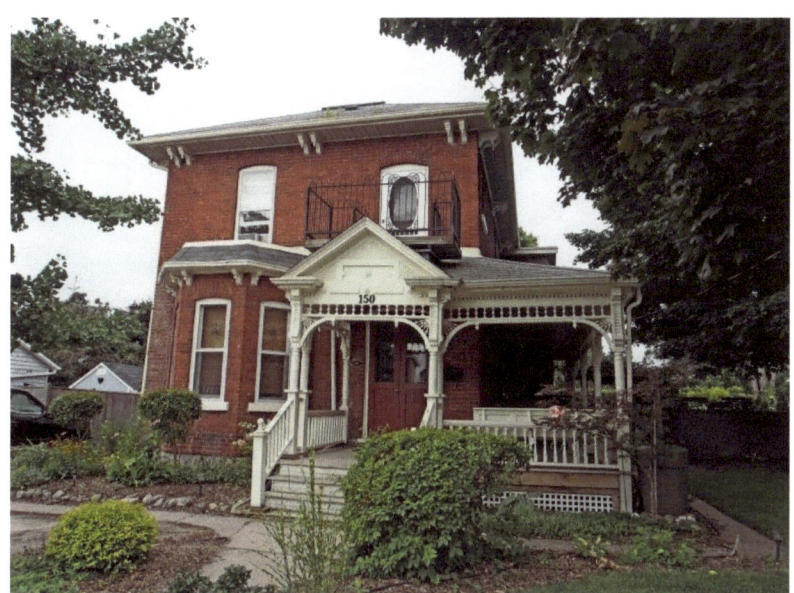

150 Sydenham Street East – Italianate, paired cornice brackets, bay window, wraparound porch – Aylmer Book 2

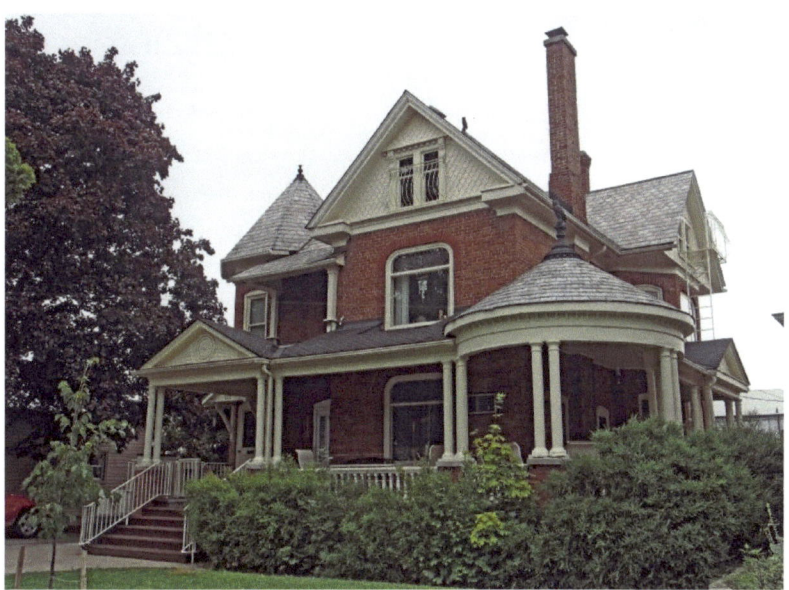

111 Sydenham Street East – Queen Anne style, turret – Aylmer Book 2

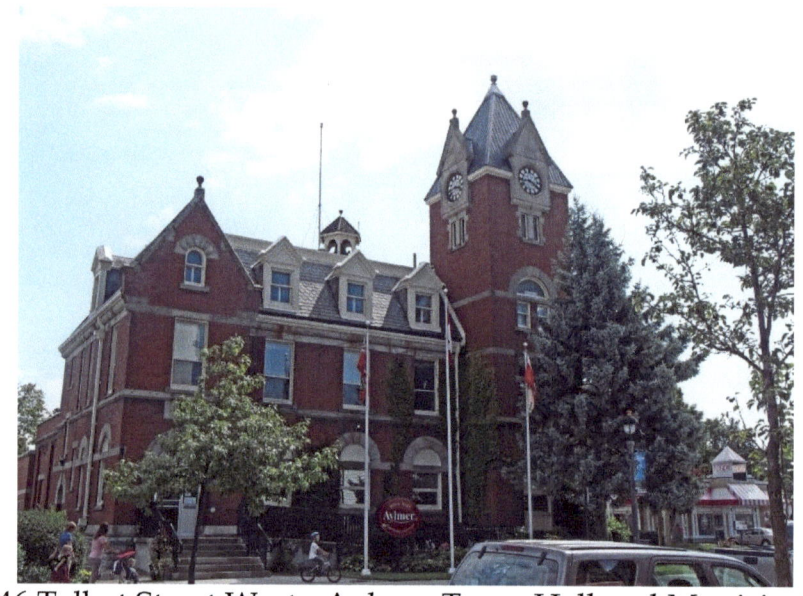

46 Talbot Street West - Aylmer Town Hall and Municipal Offices – clock tower, dormers, cupola, arched window voussoirs – Aylmer Book 2

Drayton, Ontario and area – My Top 6 Picks

Centre Wellington is a township in south-central Ontario. The primary communities in the township are Elora and Fergus. Some of the smaller communities are **Alma, Salem, and Speedside.**

Parker was a settlement in Ontario, located along the Elora-Saugeen road. Settlers moved to the area to begin new lives and to farm. To provide accommodation for travelers in horse-drawn vehicles, a hotel opened in 1850. In 1865, Thomas Burns opened a post office which brought a few neighboring businesses to the area. As travel became more modern, the need for overnight stay diminished and the town began to dwindle. It is still used for farming today but the hotel and post office have closed. The school house is still standing and is a private home, painted pink.

Conestogo Lake Conservation Area is in the heart of Mennonite country. It is on a y-shaped lake that stretches six kilometres up each arm. A unique feature of this area is the huge concrete flood control dam and reservoir surrounded by large tracts of forest, giving the appearance that the park is in northern Ontario. This is a multi-recreational-use park for camping, power boating, sailing, water skiing, canoeing and fishing.

Glen Allan is located in Wellington County southeast of Conestogo Lake.

Yatton is located in Wellington County. The area was settled by people in the early 1820s, when Black Loyalists, African-Canadians and African-American immigrants arrived in the wilderness of the Queen's Bush. Until the late 1840s the Queen's Bush remained an unorganized territory. Three African-Canadian churches were constructed in the Queen's Bush and one of them was in Yatton which Reverend Samuel H. Brown established on his farm.

Drayton is a community in Wellington County. The village is on the corner of Wellington Road 8 and Wellington Road 11, and is located northwest of Fergus and southwest of Arthur.

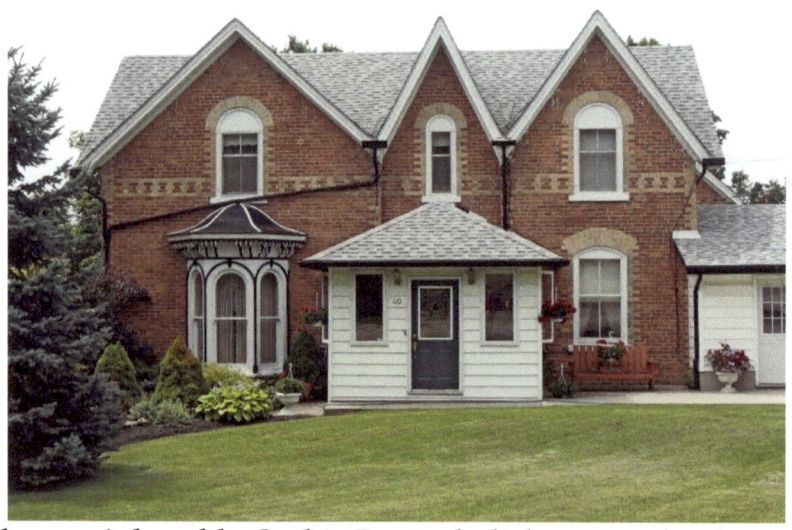

Alma - triple gable Gothic Revival, dichromatic brickwork, bay window, arched window voussoirs

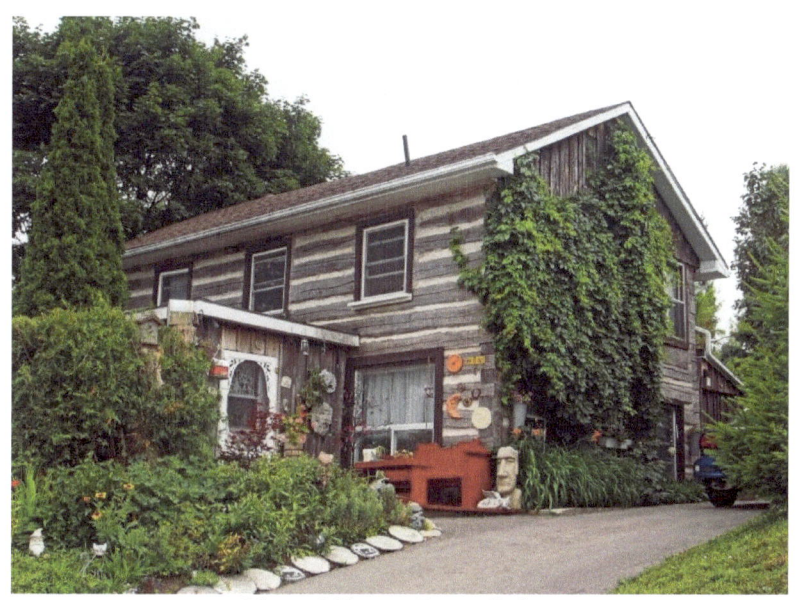

Glen Allan - Log Cabin

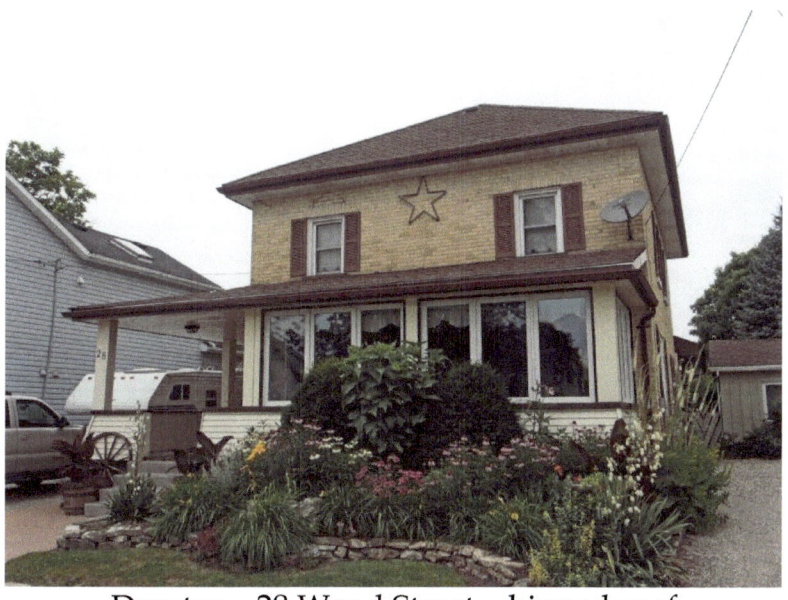

Drayton - 28 Wood Street – hipped roof

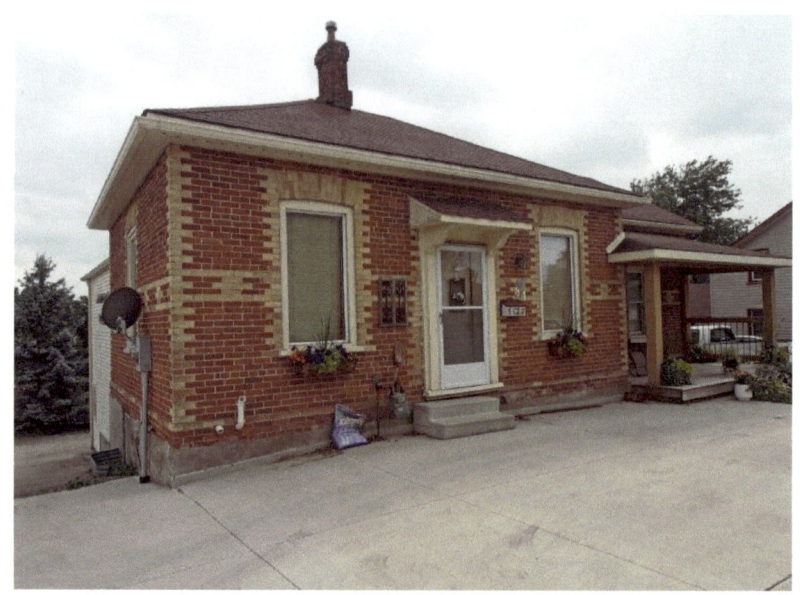
81 John Street – dichromatic brickwork

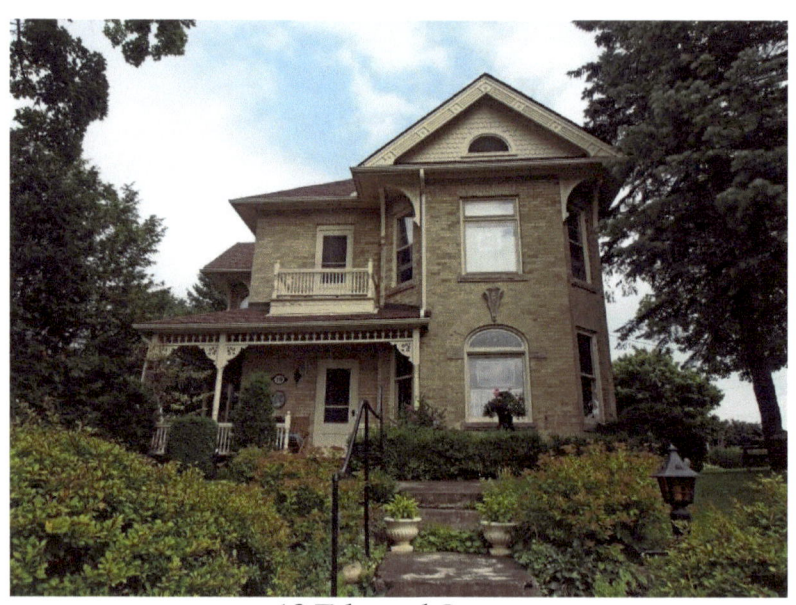
19 Edward Street

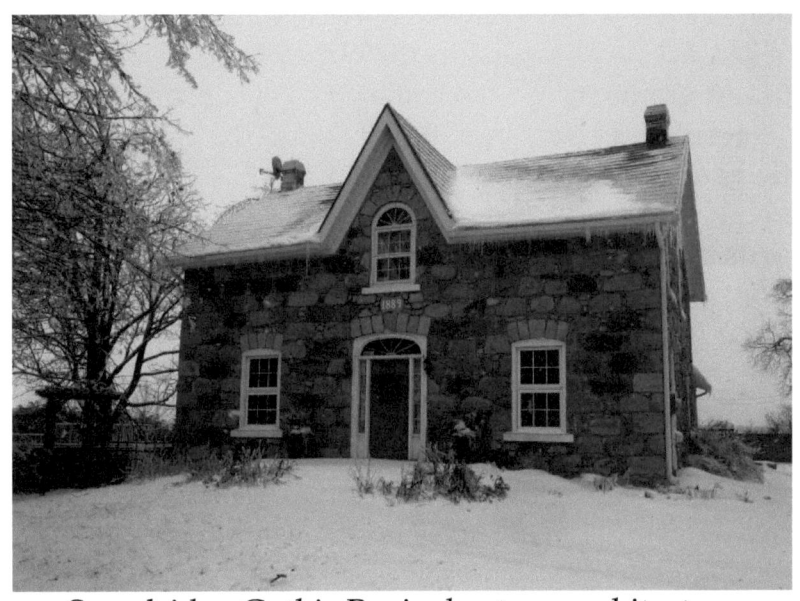

Speedside - Gothic Revival - stone architecture

Tillsonburg, Ontario – My Top 5 Picks

Tillsonburg is a town in Oxford County located about 50 kilometers southeast of London on Highway 3 at the junction of Highway 19 which connects to Highway 401.

The area was settled in 1825 by George Tillson and other immigrants from Massachusetts. A forge and sawmill were erected and roads built which led to the establishment of a settlement on the Big Otter Creek originally called Dereham Forge.

In 1836 the village was renamed Tillsonburg in honor of its founder. It was also in this year that the main street, Broadway, was laid out to its full 100-foot (30 meter) width. Because the village was predominantly a logging and wood product center, the street width was to accommodate the turning of three-team logging wagons. This width has become a benefit toward handling the pressures of modern-day traffic by providing angled parking. The extension of Broadway north was called Plank Line and is now known as Highway 19.

The water system supplied pure water for domestic use, and provided water power to such industries as a sawmill, planing mill, grist mill, spinning mill, pottery and a tannery. Many of these new establishments were owned, started, or financed by George Tillson.

In 1915, a Public Library was built with funds provided by the Carnegie Foundation, and the town's Memorial Hospital was constructed in 1925. In the 1920s, major enterprises included milk production, manufacture of shoes, tractors, textiles and tobacco.

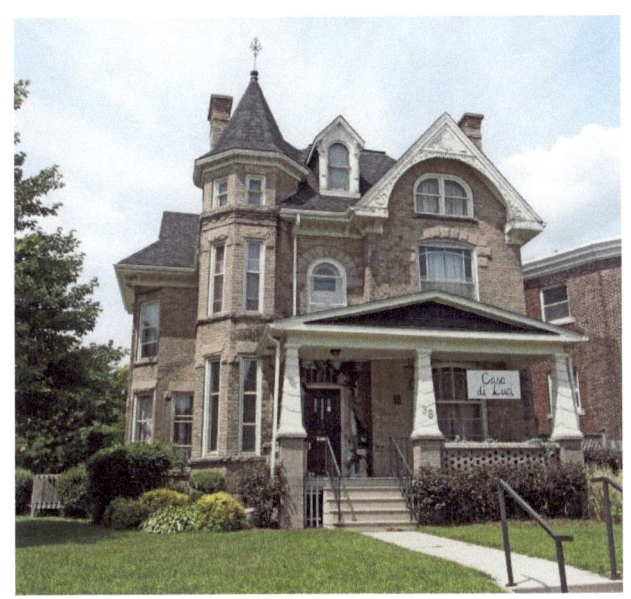

38 Ridout Street West - Casa di Luca Restaurant - Queen Anne style, verge board trim on gable, turret

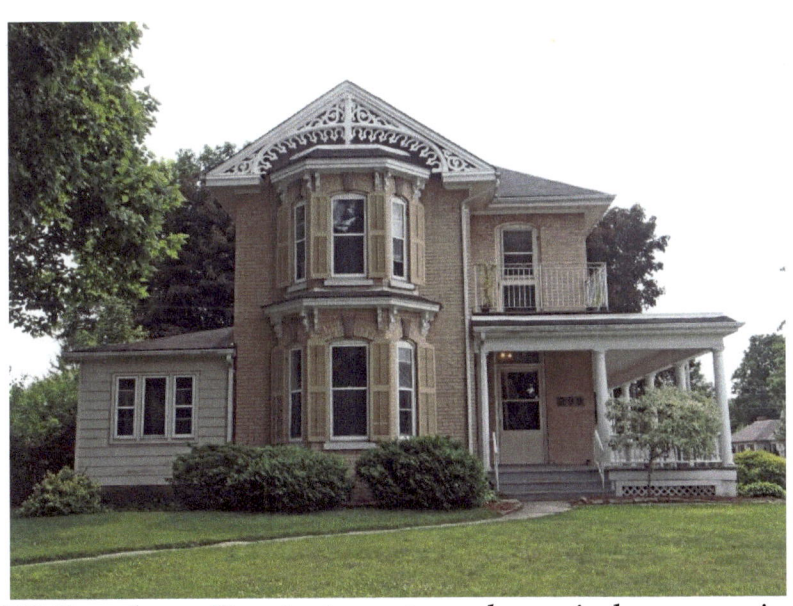

299 Broadway Street – two-storey bay windows, cornice brackets, verge board trim

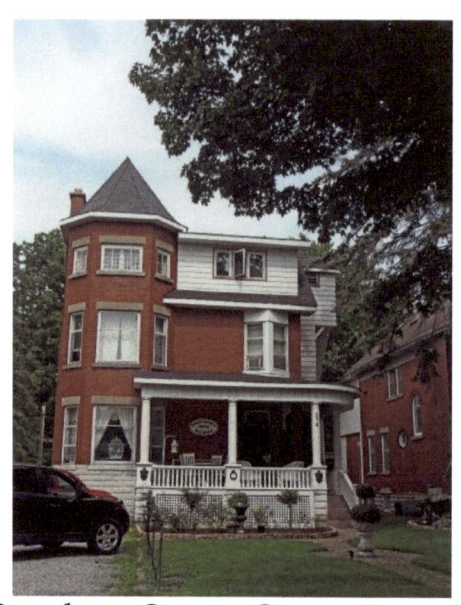

276 Broadway Street - Queen Anne, turret

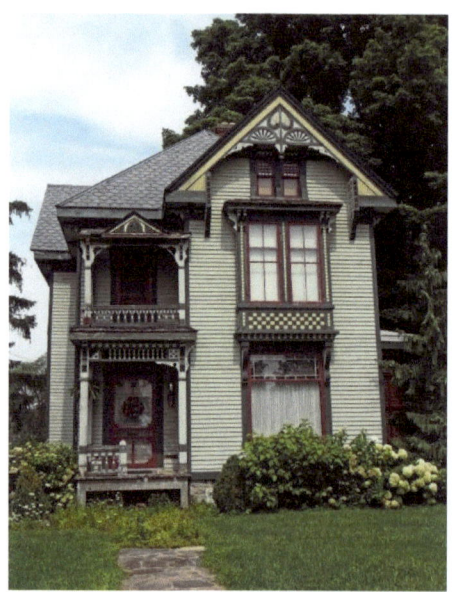

300 Broadway Street – verge board trim

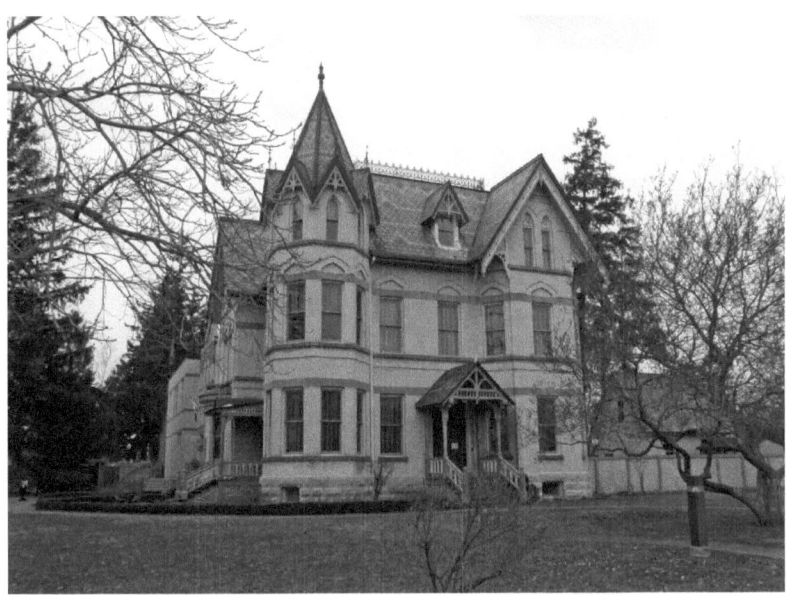

30 Tillson Avenue – Annandale National Historic Site - Constructed in seven years in the 1880s, this was the farm house for E.D. Tillson's 600 acre Model Farm. The interior of the house exemplifies the Victorian style of design known as the "Aesthetic Art Movement" which was popularized by Oscar Wilde, and encouraged the use of color and decorative detailing. There are hand-painted ceilings, elaborate inlaid floors, ornate mantles, and stained glass throughout.

Arthur, Ontario – My Top 9 Picks

(There are so many beautiful old homes in Arthur that it was difficult to choose only a few.)

Arthur is located just north of Highway 6 and Wellington Road 109 in the township of Wellington North.

Arthur, named for Arthur Wellesley, Duke of Wellington, was the southern terminus of the Garafraxa "colonization road" to Owen Sound. Settlers arrived in 1840 with the town site being officially surveyed in 1846. The establishment of saw and grist mills hastened growth in the community which was also the natural market center for the area's agricultural production.

In 1851 a post office was opened and the first church and school were organized. A weekly newspaper, The Arthur Enterprise News, began publication in 1863 and a Division Court met at Arthur. In 1872, a station of the Toronto Grey and Bruce Railway was opened in the community.

In 1897, Arthur was one of the first villages in Ontario to be served by a power transmission line. There were no meters, but people were charged ten cents for each light bulb used. Power was available in the evenings and was cut off at midnight.

James Morrison, an influential activist in farmers' causes, lived two kilometers south of Arthur. He entered politics in the early 1900s, a time when many farmers felt ignored in an increasingly urban and industrial society. Morrison helped form the United Farmers of Ontario (UFO) and the United Farmers' Cooperative in 1914. Morrison advocated cooperative effort among farmers.

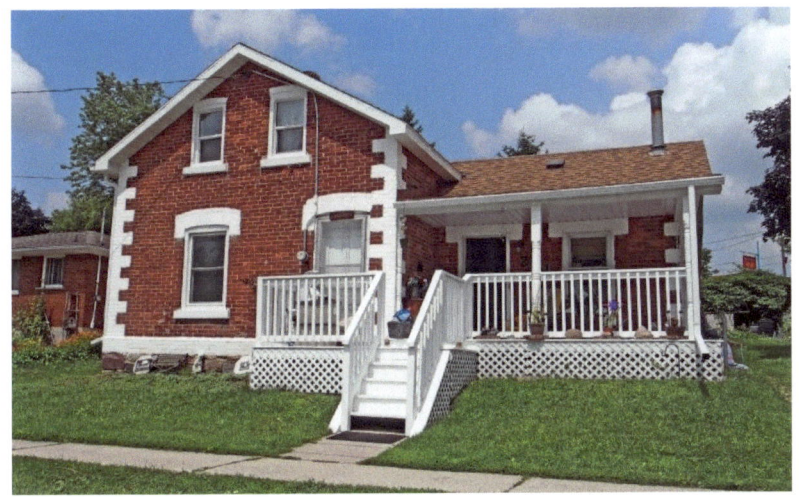

Gothic Revival, corner quoins

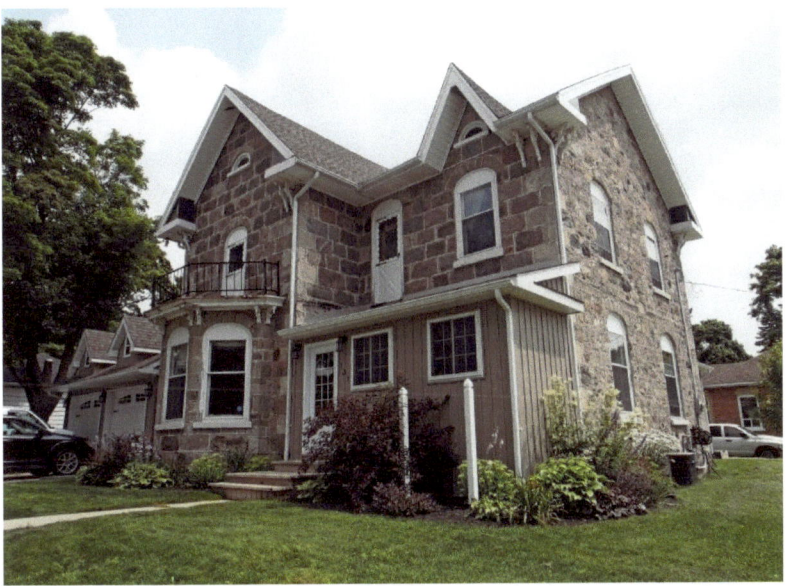

131 Frederick Street West - Gothic Revival, stone architecture, cornice brackets, cornice return on gables

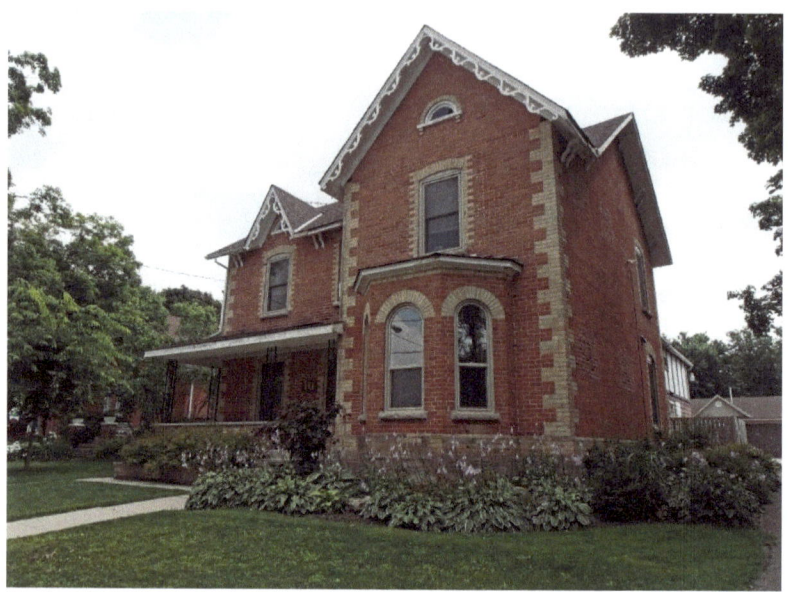

111 Frederick Street West – Gothic Revival, verge board trim on gables, corner quoins

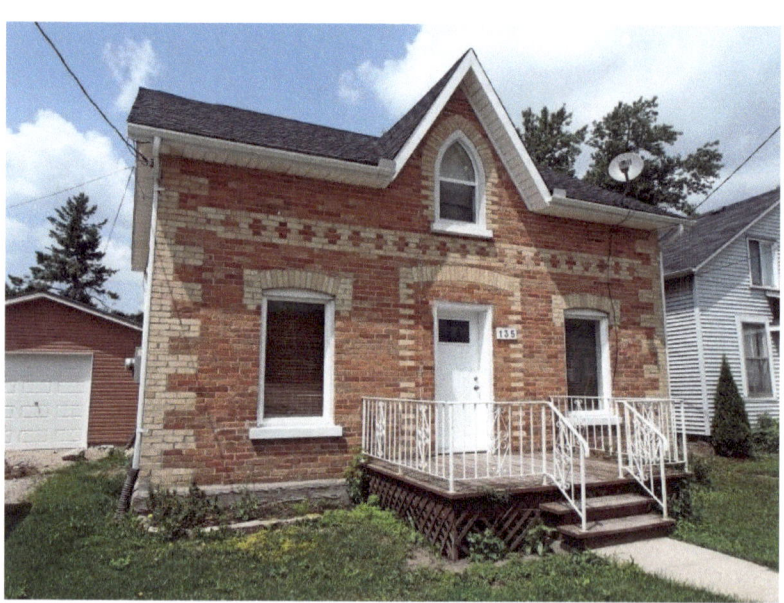

135 Frederick Street West – Gothic Revival, dichromatic brickwork, corner quoins

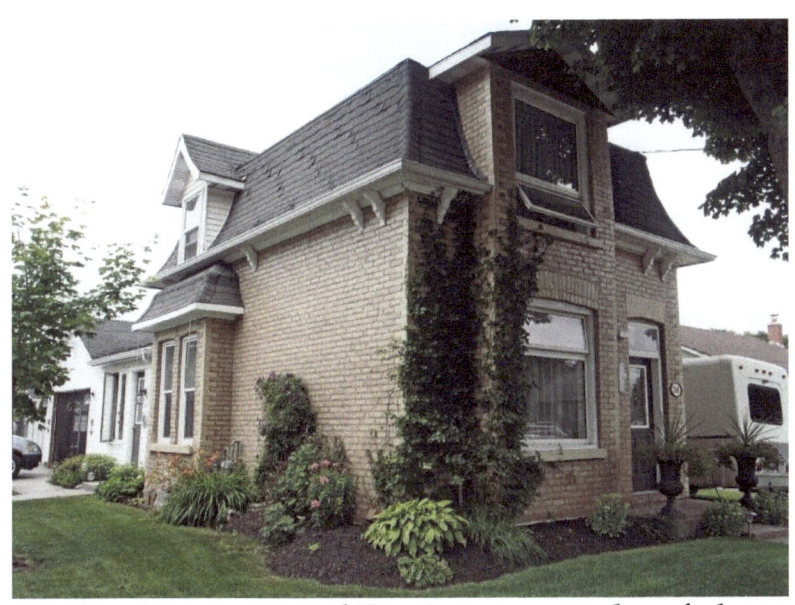

261 Tucker Street – Second Empire – mansard roof, dormers, cornice brackets

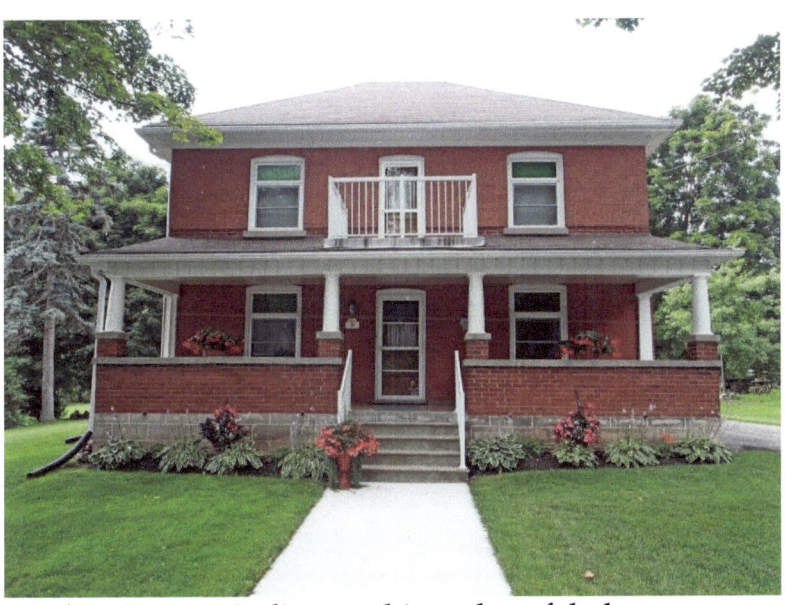

171 Tucker Street – Italianate, hipped roof, balcony on second floor

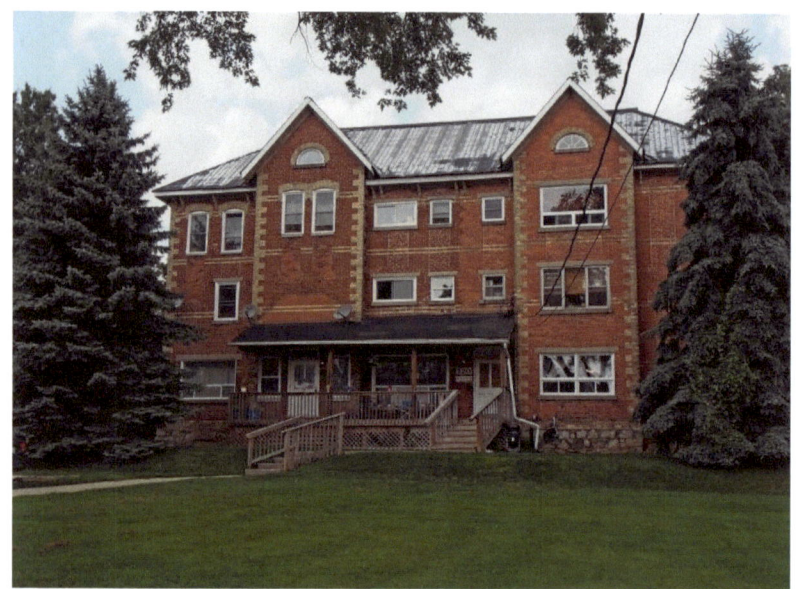

220 Smith Street – corner quoins, 3½ storey tower-like bays

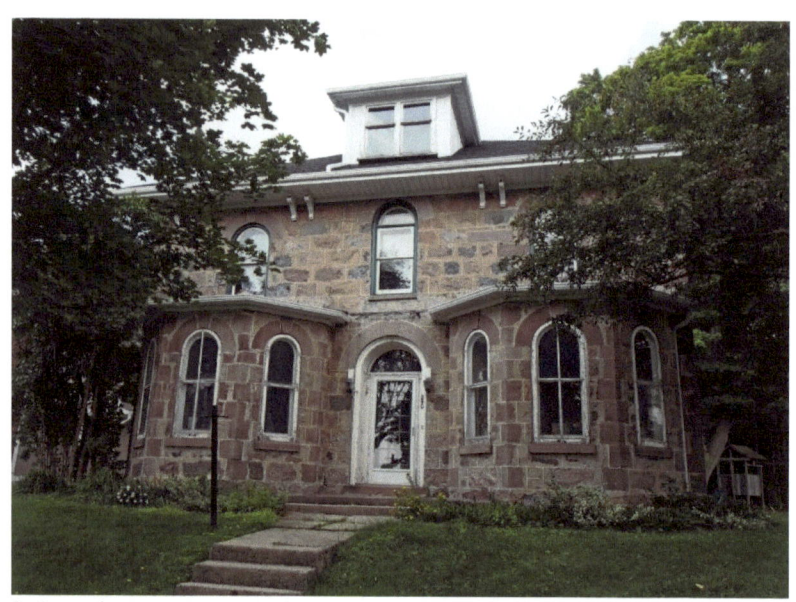

240 Smith Street – Bellview – A.D. 1887 - stone architecture, bay windows, dormer on roof, paired cornice brackets

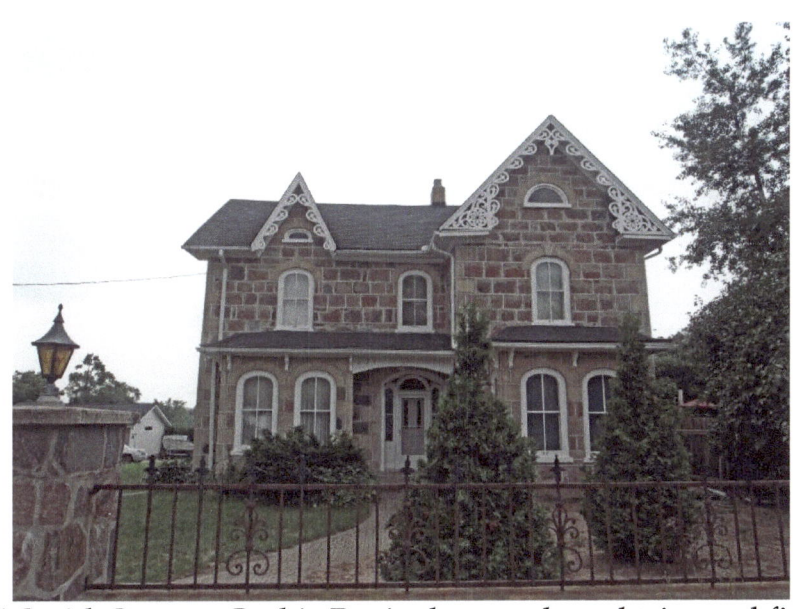

271 Smith Street – Gothic Revival, verge board trim and finial on gables, stone architecture, bay windows, cornice brackets

Rockwood, Ontario – My Top 4 Picks

Rockwood is located on Highway 7 between Acton and the city of Guelph. The Eramosa River runs through the center of the village.

Early settlers to this area were Quakers. John Harris, the first settler, erected a shanty in 1821. In 1840 Colonel Henry Strange settled and brought further development to the area which became known as Strange's Mills. Strange was the Deputy Provincial Surveyor and he opened a lime quarry which provided stone for building mills. In the 1850s the community became known as Rockwood which reflected the lovely river valley, mixed forest, high rocky hills, and geological potholes. The Eramosa River provided power for John Gamble's sawmill which was the first in Wellington County. Grist, flour, oatmeal, stave, and woollen mills followed. A post office was opened in 1853 and the Grand Trunk Railway opened a station in 1855.

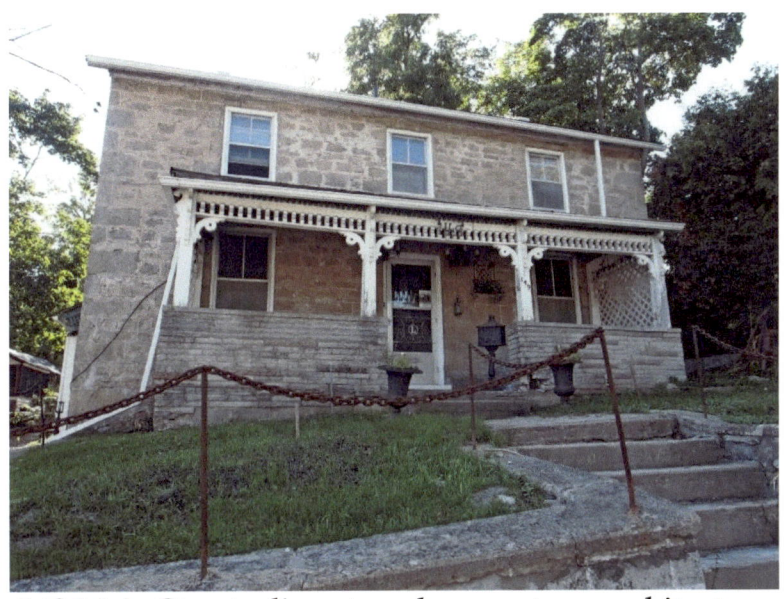

149 Main Street – limestone house, stone architecture

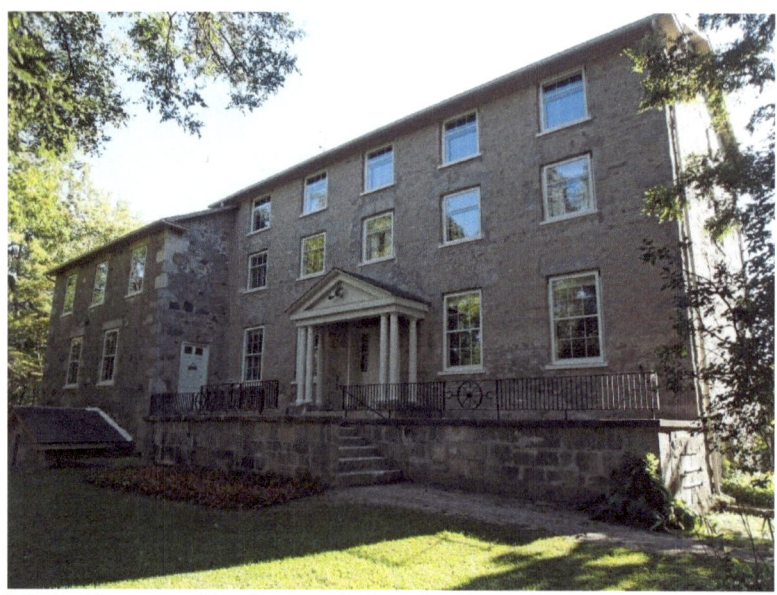

477 Main Street – Rockwood Academy - Georgian style - three-storey stone building with limestone walls, rough-cut quoins, symmetrical five-bay façade with double-hung six-over-six wood sash windows with a central door with a portico and a transom window and sidelights. It has a low-pitched cedar-shingle gable roof with many small brick and stone chimneys. The owner's bedrooms still exist on the second floor, as do the students' bedrooms on the third floor. The south wing still has the classroom below the student bedrooms. The west wing remains unaltered and contains a carriage house on the ground floor with a gymnasium above.

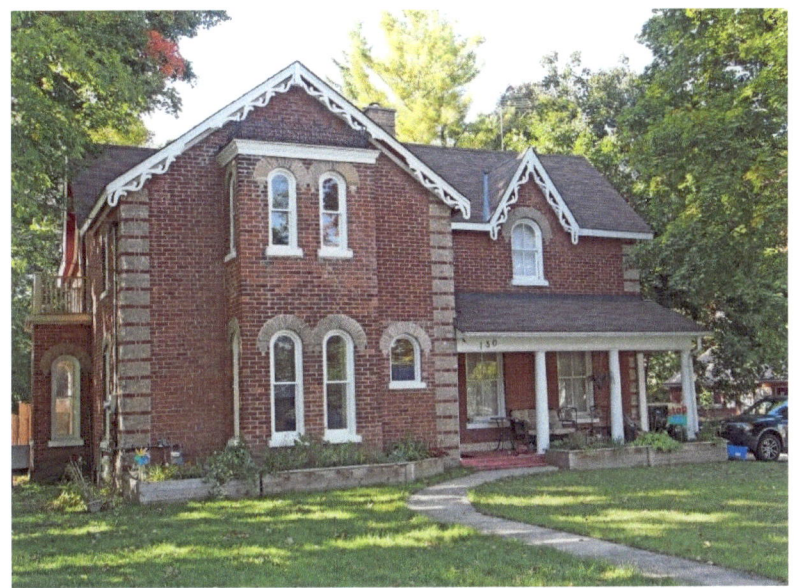

130 Guelph Street – Gothic Revival, verge board trim on gables, corner quoins, arched voussoirs, two-storey tower-like bay

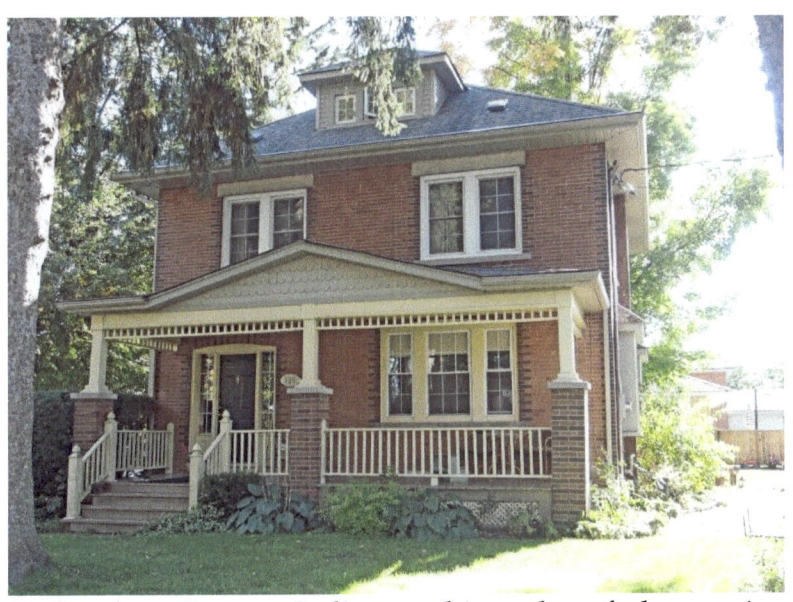

125 Richardson Street – Italianate, hipped roof, dormer in attic

Acton, Ontario – My Top 8 Picks

Acton is located at the intersection of Highway 7 and Halton Regional Road 25. Methodist preachers Ezra and Zenas Adams and their brother Rufus settled on the west branch of the Credit River in the 1820s. A community of pioneer families grew around the Adams family farms. Nicklin's saw and grist mill and Nelles' tannery operated here by the early 1840s.

Acton was first named Danville when Settler Wheeler Green opened a dry-goods store in 1828. It was later called Adamsville, after the early settlers. In 1846, the postmaster named the community after the area of Acton in West London, England.

Tanning was an important industry in Acton from 1844 when the first tannery was established. The area was attractive to the leather industry because of the large numbers of trees. Acton was known as the leather capital of Canada. At the turn of the century, it was the largest tanning center in the British Empire. The tannery continued in operation until its closure in September 1986.

The town's location was chosen because of the good source of waterpower from the Black Creek, and the flour mill established at the beginning is still in operation today, although its source of power has changed. Acton is near the watershed between the Credit River and the Grand River which is just west of the urban area where the Blue Springs Creek begins.

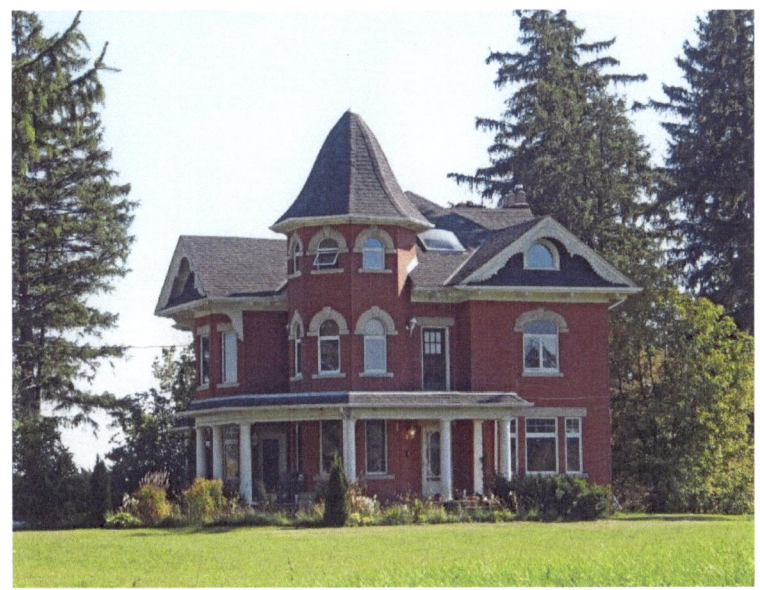

Queen Anne style, three storey turret, architraves with keystones, verge board trim on gables, fretwork, ionic pillars

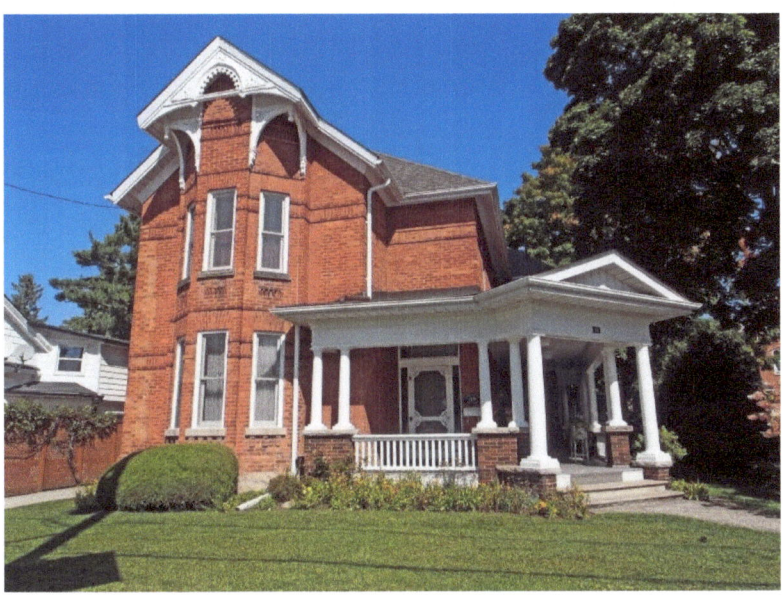

39 Willow Street – Knox Manse established 1889 – Italianate with two-and-a-half storey tower-like bay, pediment above pillared porch, fretwork and verge board on gable

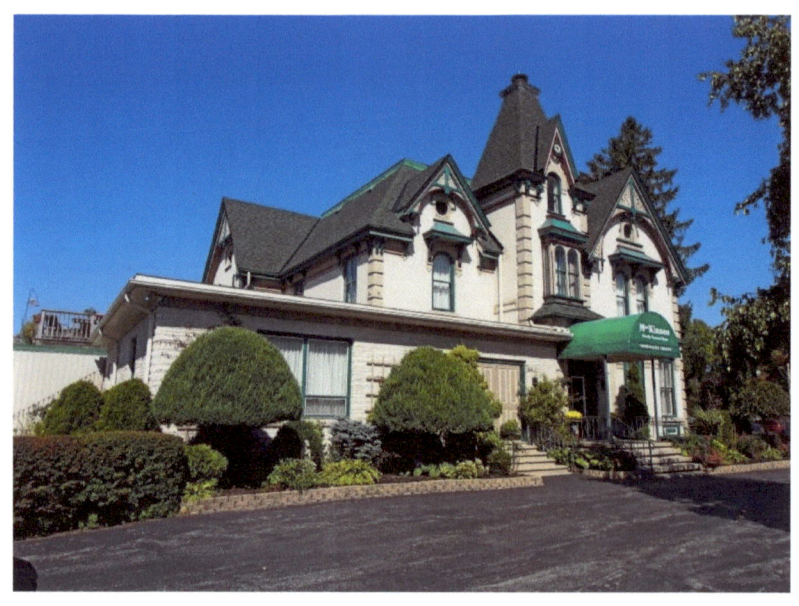

55 Mill Street East was built in 1879 by William H. Storey who came to Canada as a child in 1845 and came to Acton in 1856 as a saddle apprentice. He branched out on his own and eventually owned the Storey Glove Factory which was located on Bower Avenue (where the Post Office is now). He built this beautiful Victorian Home at 55 Mill Street East for his family. It was called "The Sunderland Villa". His carriage house was located at 7 John Street and he heated the carriage house and his home via underground steam pipes from the factory. Mr. Storey died in 1898. After the First World War the building was used to house soldiers and then sat derelict for a number of years until Victor Rumley purchased it in 1937 and moved The MacKinnon Family Funeral Home with Shoemaker Chapel to this location.

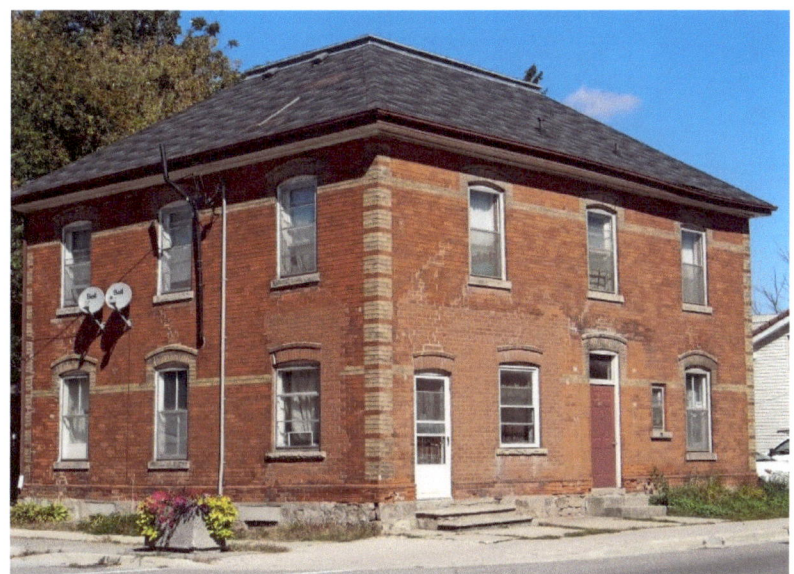

105 Mill Street – Italianate, hipped roof, corner quoins, banding

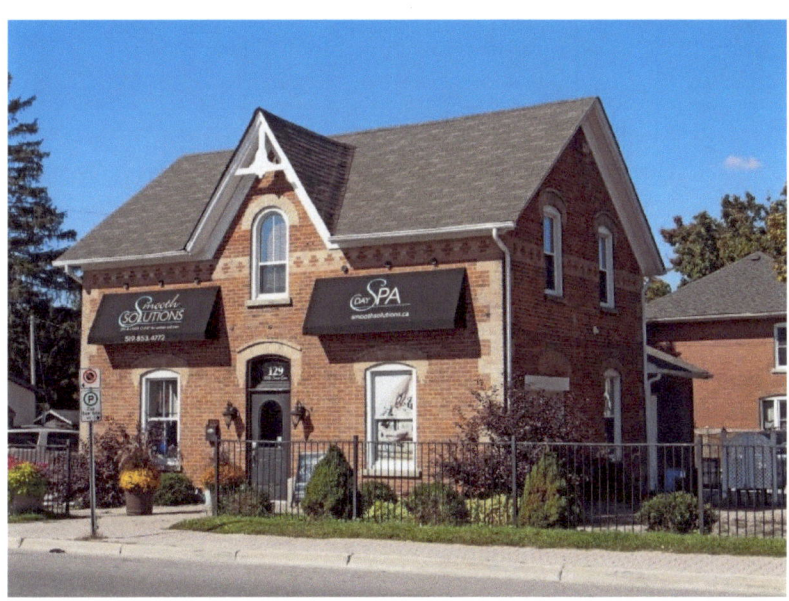

129 Mill Street – Gothic Revival, dichromatic brickwork, corner quoins

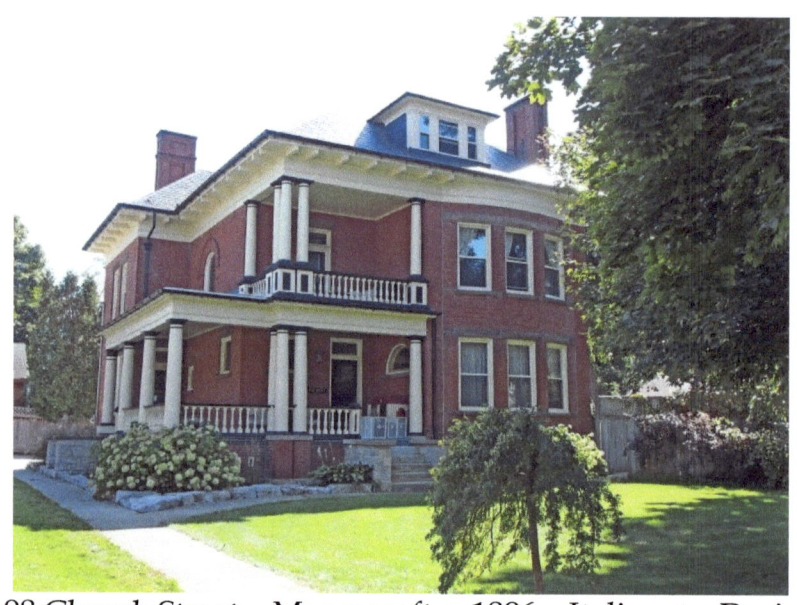

98 Church Street – Moorecroft c. 1896 – Italianate, Doric pillars, dormer in attic, wraparound verandah on lower level, pillared balcony on second floor

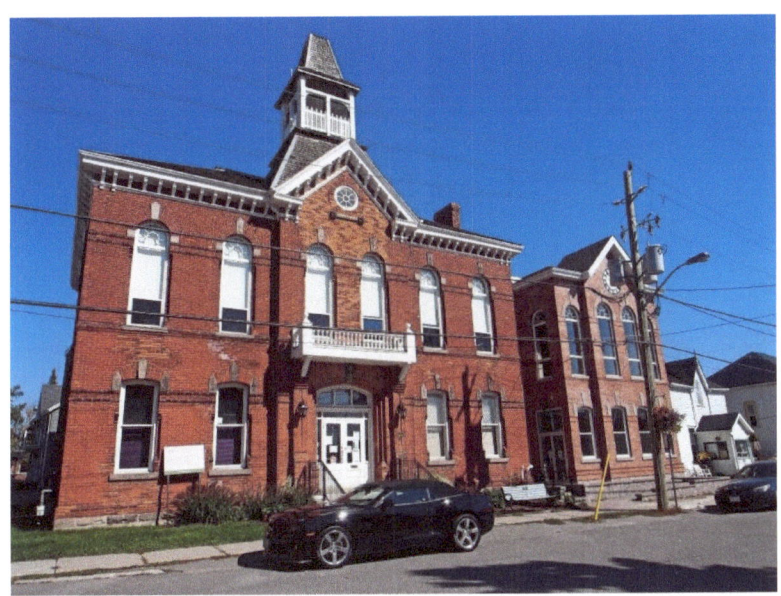

19 Willow Street North - Acton Town Hall opened in 1883 with a grand ball and remained the hub of Acton's social life for over 80 years. The upstairs auditorium was used for meetings, dances, concerts, Sunday School plays, amateur dramatics, and minstrel shows. The police station, council chambers, library, and practice room for the Acton Citizens' Band were housed downstairs. In 1974 the regional government moved out of Acton to Georgetown. It is in the Italianate style with cornice brackets, cupola, arched voussoirs with keystones over the windows, cornice return on the gable of the two-and-a-half storey frontispiece; sidelights and transom windows around the front door.

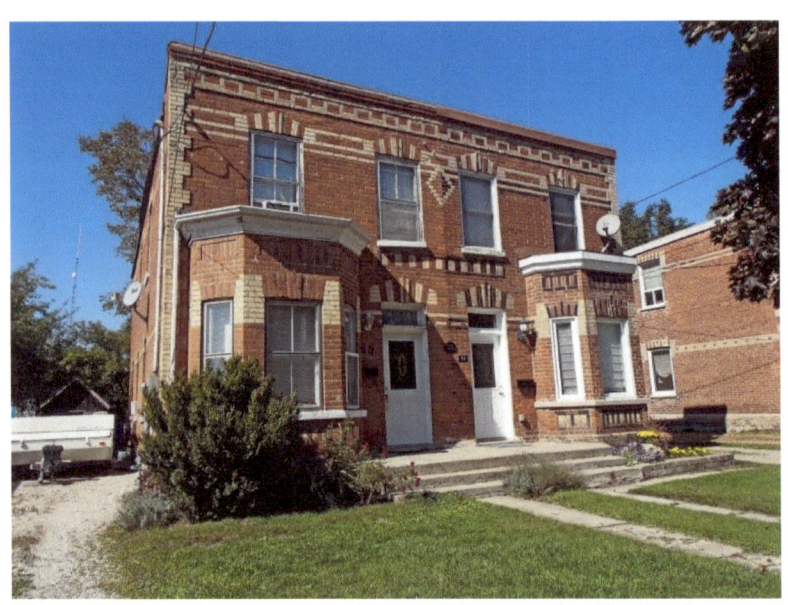

69-71 Bower Street - Syndicate Houses built 1882 – Five double houses were built by the Acton Building Association as tenements for workers. Each is remarkable for its distinctive brick pattern

Orillia, Ontario – My Top 5 Picks

Orillia is located in Central Ontario between Lake Couchiching and Lake Simcoe, 135 kilometers (84 miles) north of Toronto. Both lakes are part of the Trent-Severn Waterway. Travel north on Lake Couchiching, then through three locks and the only marine railway in North America leads to Georgian Bay on Lake Huron. Travelling south-east across Lake Simcoe, through many locks (including two of the highest hydraulic lift locks in the world) eventually leads to Lake Ontario. From either of these Great Lakes one can connect to the St. Lawrence and then to the Atlantic Ocean.

Due to logging and rail links with Toronto and Georgian Bay, Orillia became a commercial center and summer resort in the mid-1800s. William Tudhope opened a blacksmith shop in 1864 at Andrew and Colborne Streets. By the end of the century, William's son James headed the Tudhope Carriage Company as part of a conglomerate of businesses. In 1866, Thomas Mulcahy launched his mercantile career in dry goods with the opening of his California Store. Mulcahy and his sons were responsible for the construction of many of Orillia's dwellings and commercial buildings. Andrew Tait was the President of the Huntsville Lumber Company. Tait was a major employer and said to be Orillia's first millionaire.

Across Lake Couchiching, John Thomson opened his Longford saw milling operation in 1868, using Orillia as a shipping base. By 1900, Orillia was one of the most bustling towns in Ontario. Many of the commercial and residential buildings erected and still standing used red brick trimmed with limestone quarried from Longford.

The town boasted the best Opera House north of Toronto and industrial growth almost unparalleled in the province. With the expansion of the railways, thousands arrived each summer for picnics and holidaying at Couchiching Park.

In 1912, Orillia was the first municipality in North America to introduce daylight saving time and had the first municipal hydro electric transmission plant in North America. This energy powered an industrial boom with sawmills, iron foundries, and a host of manufacturing companies producing farm implements, carriages, and automobiles and shipping these products across Canada.

In Stephen Leacok's 1912 book *Sunshine Sketches of a Little Town*, Orillia was used as the basis for the fictional town known as "Mariposa". The book was based on Leacock's experiences in the town and the city has since the book's release attempted to mimic the fictional location in as many ways as possible. Orillia is known as the "Sunshine City". The Stephen Leacock Museum is a National Historic Site in Orillia.

William E. Bell's 1989 novel *Five Days of the Ghost* was set in Orillia with many readers recognizing popular local spots, including the Guardian Angels Catholic Church, the Samuel de Champlain statue in Couchiching Beach Park and Big Chief Island in the middle of Lake Couchiching. Orillia is also known as the birthplace of Gordon Lightfoot.

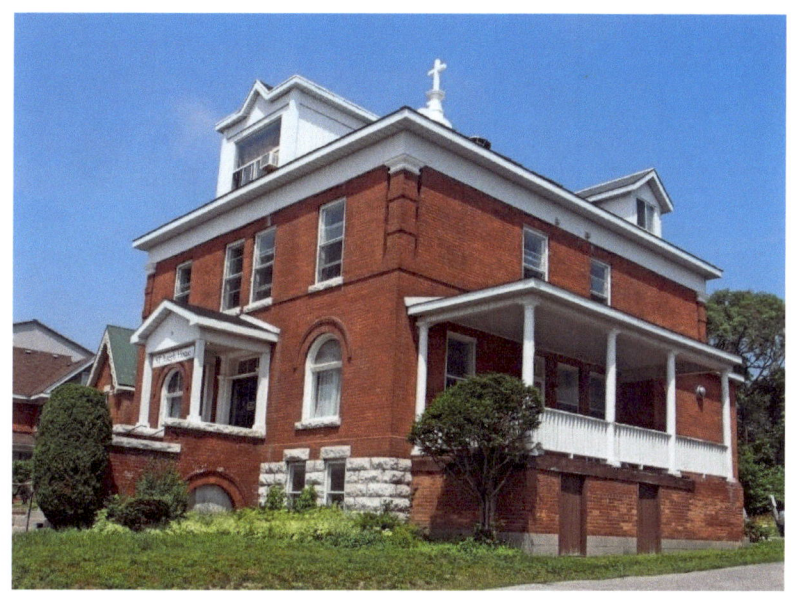

24 Penetang Street – St. Joseph House - Catholic Family Services of Simcoe County

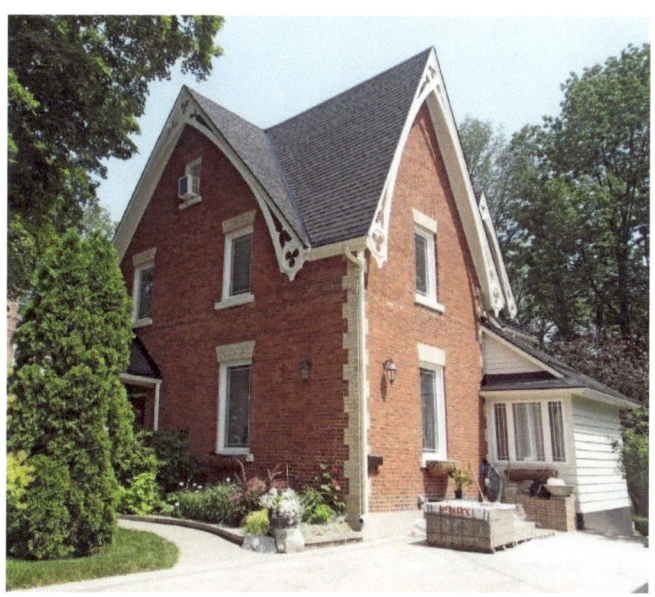

Gothic Revival, verge board trim, corner quoins

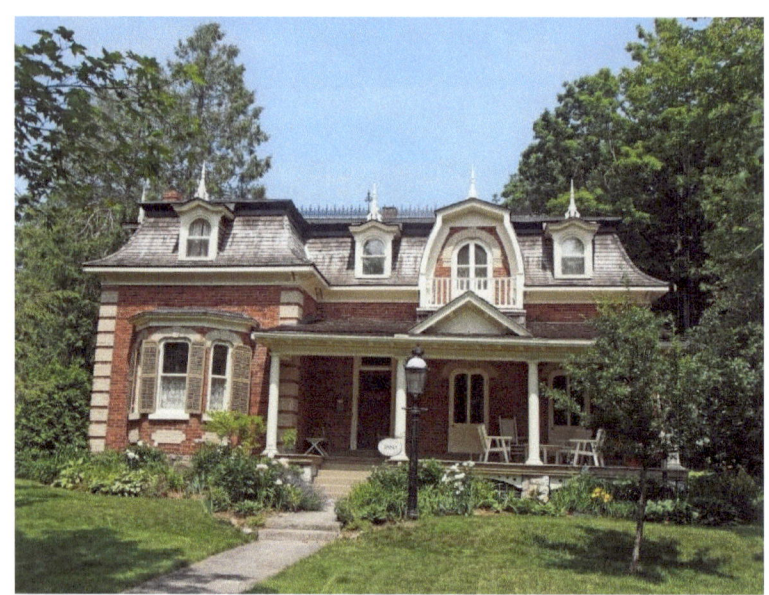

84 Brant Street East – E.J. McCrohan, Harness Maker c. 1880 - Second Empire style, mansard roof, iron cresting around roof, finials on dormers, second floor balcony, corner quoins

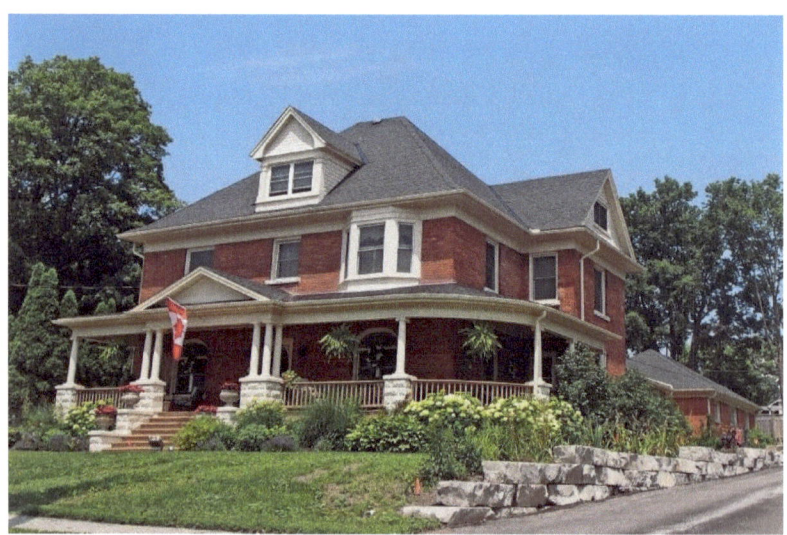

Dormer in attic, pediment above wraparound verandah, second floor bay window

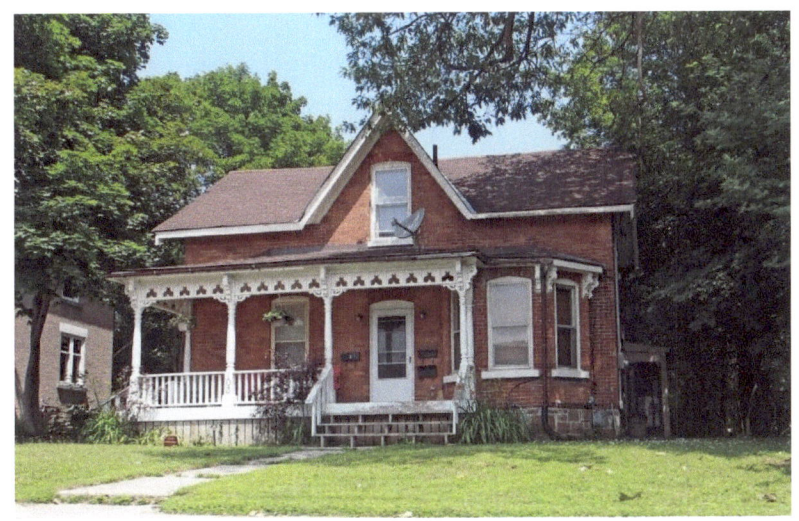

#106 – Gothic Revival, cornice brackets

www.ingramcontent.com/pod-product-compliance
Lightning Source LLC
Chambersburg PA
CBHW040225220526
45473CB00001B/128